W9-BMH-793

TRAINING THE STREET℠

© 1999–2016 Training The Street, Inc.
All rights reserved.

Preparing Financial Professionals for Success
www.trainingthestreet.com

123115

Table of Contents

Congratulations on acquiring to Training The Street's **TTS Financial Modeling**. Training The Street (TTS for short) is the world's foremost provider of instructor-led courses in financial modeling and valuation training. We work with Wall Street investment banks, Fortune 500 companies, business schools, and colleges.

This self-study book is a response to a need many of you have expressed—a need for a course pack you could use on your own if you could not attend one of our live classes. What you have in your hands is the very best out-of-classroom experience possible—a distillation of all the knowledge we've gained from training thousands of professionals and students in live seminars. This is a complete, self-contained course. You won't need any other resources to become proficient at Excel-based core financial modeling. Welcome aboard, and let's get started.

1.1 WHO IS THIS COURSE FOR?

First off, you don't have to work on Wall Street—or be planning to—in order to benefit from this course. Financial modeling has a vast range of applications, and our course is designed for professionals and students from many backgrounds and with very different goals. We've focused on transferable skills and techniques that can be applied in a diverse range of industries and businesses. For sure, these include traditional areas such as investment banking, investment research, and sales and trading, but financial modeling is also used in:

- **Consulting** – Financial models help management and strategy consultants develop and deliver value-added advice to their clients.

- **Industry Finance** – Financial modeling is used extensively in the internal finance departments of companies ranging from small technology start-ups to large multinationals.

- **Retail Industry** – Managers use models to forecast volumes and trends both on the buy side (for example, a fashion buyer) and on the sell side (for example, a fashion label).

- **Accounting** – Models are critical in preparing and auditing financial statements.

This package is designed for:

- People new to modeling,
- Intermediate modelers, and
- Experienced modelers.

New to modeling – Perhaps you are transitioning to a job that requires financial modeling skills or preparing for an interview where you will be tested on modeling. If you're new to Excel-based financial modeling, don't worry. You'll find that our materials provide an intuitive, step-by-step approach. Regardless of your comfort level with the subject, we will be there to walk you through the challenges. We've seen them a thousand times in our live classes, and we've figured out the clearest and quickest ways to get these concepts across to you.

Intermediate modelers – Perhaps it's been a while since you last built a financial model. You can use this guide as a quick refresher, or to introduce yourself to a different application of modeling. There are plenty of sophisticated challenges in this how-to guide to sharpen the skills of the intermediate user.

Experienced modelers – If you're already an experienced financial modeler, you'll very likely find some new ideas throughout this book that will make you faster and more efficient and equip you with a more powerful and logical approach.

1.2 HOW IS THIS COURSE ORGANIZED?

With years of professional teaching experience behind us, we have assembled what we believe is *the* optimal way to teach you financial modeling.

The course pack you have in your hands teaches you how to construct an integrated financial model from scratch. It assumes you have very limited knowledge in financial model building. In the appropriate sections, it also introduces you to Excel-based best practices.

> *Included in the Financial Modeling Course Pack are the Self-Study Book, Case Studies and an Online Companion.*

The course pack blends a traditional hard-copy book format with Excel templates and online media. In each case, the hard-copy book is a resource guide you can access even when you are away from your computer. The Excel exercises, templates, and model reinforce the concepts covered in the books. For trickier concepts and modeling techniques, we offer a library of online media designed to walk you through these more difficult topics and to illustrate efficiencies. Our online media library is continually updated with the latest software, functionality, and support.

SPECIAL FEATURES

 Multimedia – *This icon indicates that you can find multimedia clips in the Online Companion. Please log in to the website to view the Online Companion. You can pause to watch the multimedia clips and then return to the book.*

 Key Formulas – *To accelerate your learning, we have also identified key formulas we regard as especially critical to financial modeling. You will recognize them by the "key" icon next to them.*

 Excel Shortcut – *We are big fans of using shortcut keys! It makes you more efficient. For more tips and tricks, we recommend purchasing our Excel Best Practices Course Pack.*

1.3 OPTIMIZING THE WAY YOU USE THIS COURSE

Throughout this guide, you will encounter practical, how-to questions aimed at keeping you focused and helping you get the most out of the course. Some examples:

- Have you ever seen this particular type of model? Can you use it in your current or future job?

- There are often different ways to accomplish a given modeling task. Can you imagine a different way of doing this particular task?

- As you examine the structural details of the model you are building, can you discern a predictable sequence in it? Can you apply that sequence? This question gets you to 'play architect' and to take a "Big Picture" view.

- Can you perform this task or build this model faster? One thing that separates advanced modelers from intermediate modelers is their ability to create a model quickly and efficiently.

- Now that you've worked on modeling a bit, can you time yourself? A clock is the "bathroom scale" of modeling. This guide will push you to find the most efficient ways to complete modeling tasks. It's the only way to improve.

  - How long does it take you to complete the whole model? A seasoned financial modeler could complete the following model in just a few hours.

 Please view the Online Companion for related supplementary media.

1.4 WHAT EXACTLY IS A FINANCIAL MODEL?

A financial model is a simplified, mathematical representation of a company's financial and operational performance over a number of historical (past) and projected (future) periods. Business professionals use models to predict the outcome of a financial decision or to forecast how a company will respond to various hypothetical economic events.

Typically, to get a sense of past trends a financial modeler examines three years of historical data. The reason for this is practical: Most public companies provide three years of information in their annual financial disclosures. But the length of the projection period ultimately depends on what the model will be used for. For example:

1. Are you an equity research analyst trying to get a sense of the company's immediate future? Then you may need to forecast its earnings using a 3- to 5-year projection model.

2. Or do you need, instead, to be able to assess a company's future performance or value when it matures and reaches a steady state of growth? Then your projection model may need to forecast the next 5 to 10 years. Indeed, you may need an even longer-term model if you are forecasting a "growth" company. Growth companies often take more than 10 years to reach steady state.

We believe generally that five years is generally an approximately long enough projection period to get a good sense of a company's immediate future. But in your real-world work, the important thing to ask yourself is what the model's purpose is. Effective modelers make every decision with this end goal in mind.

Length of projection period is just one factor, however. There are many *kinds* of models to choose from. Here are a few basic ones:

- Corporate Finance Model
  - **Earnings model/Profit and loss model**
  - Debt/Recapitalization/Financing model
  - Merger consequences model
  - Comps model
  - **Discounted cash flow model**

- Sales and Trading Model
  - Bond pricing model
  - Option pricing model

- Industry Finance Model

- Detailed budgets/Profit and loss

In this book, we will guide you through the creation of one particular type of model: **the Earnings model**. Its primary goal is to examine a company's earnings per share (EPS) and earnings per share growth over the immediate future. Why did we choose this kind of model? Several reasons:

First, it's **everywhere**: It is the most common type of model among financial practitioners. For instance, at many companies internal finance teams use it to forecast its profit and loss (P&L). Investment bankers forecast the same information, using the model to pitch value-added products and services to a client. Research analysts use it to forecast EPS to support an investment recommendation.

Second, it's **fundamental**: The earnings model is the basis for many other kinds of financial analyses, such as the **discounted cash flow (DCF) analysis** (more on this later).

And finally, it's **comprehensive**. Constructing an earnings model compels you to master all the fundamental skills you'll ever need to build and use virtually any model you're likely to encounter in your career. The skills you will acquire—or sharpen—from building the earnings model in this book include:

- Learning to lay out a model with *a specific goal in mind*,

- Mastering how to forecast performance using relationship drivers,

- Understanding how to choose reasonable, defensible assumptions in making your projections, and

- Making it second nature to adhere to modeling best practices, including formatting standards and formula building.

Core skills you will need: Accounting

You don't need to be an accounting expert for this course, but there are a few basic accounting rules that form the foundation for modeling. Here are three critical ones:

 1. **A = L + E**. Our model must be balanced, or "in parity." This means its **asset balances** must equal the sum of its **liability** and **equity balances**, both in its historical and in projected years. After we've completed the model, we'll use a variety of techniques—including a "parity check line"—to make sure the balance sheet is in parity.

2. If a non-cash asset (for example, accounts receivable) **increases**, then the company's cash flow **decreases** (i.e., the impact is negative). Of course, if a non-cash asset decreases, the opposite is true.

3. If a non-debt liability (for example, accounts payable) **increases**, then the company's cash flow also **increases** (i.e., the impact is positive). Of course, if a non-debt liability decreases, the opposite is true. The movements in items 2 and 3 above are also commonly referred to as sources or uses of funds (or of cash funds).

These three accounting tenets are part of a larger set of principles we refer to as the **Golden Rules of Modeling**. When practitioners check a financial model, typically the first thing they do is go to the balance sheet to make sure the model is in parity (principle #1). If it isn't, then they know that somewhere in the model one or more of these basic rules was violated. What this means is that, somewhere in the model, a change on the balance sheet from one year to the next did not properly reconcile with an appropriate, corresponding change in cash flow during that period. Our goal is to make sure that your model balances once you've completed it. But you don't have to wait until the end to find out. As you build it, you'll have various safety checks along the way to guide you toward success.

 Please view the Online Companion for related supplementary media.

Core skills you will need: Corporate finance and financial statement analysis

Corporate Finance is the discipline professionals use to guide their investment decisions. There are two kinds of investment decisions—short-term and long-term.

Short-term investment decisions typically fall under "working capital management." These decisions reflect the company's corporate finance strategy for responding to changes in its short-term assets (for example, accounts receivable) and short-term liabilities (for example, accounts payable) from one period to the next. Short-term decisions must balance two things: (i) the business's short-term financing needs (for example, a need to fund inventory) and (ii) the underlying goal of every corporation: to optimize cash flows and maximize shareholder value.

By contrast, **long-term** or "capital" investment decisions reflect the company's corporate finance strategy for selecting and funding long-term projects, such as major purchases of property, plant, and equipment. Such projects are referred to as capital expenditures, or **CapEx**. But long-term projects may also include decisions about capital structure (for example, whether the firm should issue new shares to fund an acquisition or to pay down debt), about dividend policy, or about a new or existing share repurchase program.

Here is where financial modeling comes in. An expert financial modeler (who may be part of the company's own internal corporate finance team, or who may come in as an external investment banking advisor or consultant) can add value to the business by *drawing connections* between the company's corporate finance strategy and its historical and projected financials—or by *spotting discrepancies* between strategy and data.

Financial Statement Analysis is the tool that modelers use to discover and unlock this potential value. Financial statements are found primarily in a company's SEC filings—for example, its annual 10-K filing or quarterly 10-Q filing. These filings contain financial statements that hold nearly all of the relevant, publicly available information you will need to model a company's financials. Other sources of financial data include press releases and investor call transcripts. Expert modelers use these to fill in the blanks in order to build reasonable, defensible assumptions. Analyzing financial statements, along with supporting footnotes and commentary, provides the framework modelers use when they are developing the assumptions that will drive their forecasts.

Let's use an illustration: Suppose a company's short-term strategy is to reduce inventory levels to increase cash flows, yet inventories have been steadily rising and are expected to rise even further over the next several periods. Clearly, there is opportunity for improvement, yet the company may not realize this discrepancy until an alert financial modeler discovers it. A change in management strategy, or the introduction of a new product or tool, such as an inventory procurement system, could help the business get back on track.

This is an oversimplified case, but it makes the point: Identifying opportunities like this one is the first step toward adding value for your managers or for a client.

What are you trying to do? End goal of a model

When you're creating a model, it is imperative to have the end goal in mind. If you know what you're trying to achieve, you can pursue that goal more efficiently and more effectively. Our end goal is to come up with a virtual re-creation of a particular company's business that is both *flexible* and *dynamic*. What do we mean by these terms?

A *flexible* model is an adaptable one. This means that it allows you, at some future point, to expand it in order to accommodate more advanced analyses. For example, suppose our company had multiple divisions. A flexible model is one that can easily be customized to forecast the company's integrated financials based on its individual segments.

Flexibility tends to generate a second characteristic: It helps to make a model *dynamic*. A dynamic model is one that permits you to change its **assumptions** or **drivers** easily in order to reflect real or hypothetical changes within the company, in its industry, or in its macroeconomic environment. A flexible model, in other words, allows you to test different scenarios. We should, for example, be able to change our sales growth rate assumption and readily see how this affects the company's projected financial performance. A dynamic model also enables us to easily validate our accounting rules with greater ease: For instance, an increase in a non-cash asset account should produce a decrease in the company's cash flow.

Toward the end of this book, we will discuss other uses of the earnings model. For now, let's just say that *dynamism* and *flexibility* will be two core goals we'll be seeking to achieve as we build our model together.

2.1 SETTING UP A MODEL

Good versus bad models

In financial modeling, there are, as the old saying goes, many roads up the same mountain. Over time, as you model more companies in different industries, you will come to develop your own modeling style and preferences. For example, you may prefer a vertically laid-out model to the horizontal one we present in this book. In modeling, there are often no right or wrong answers. But there are certainly good and bad models! The preferences, style choices, and other modeling decisions you make are up to you, but they should reflect the three core characteristics of a good model. A good model is:

- **Realistic and robust** – It uses reasonable, defensible assumptions to make realistic projections of a company's future performance. A realistic forecast of a company's future is one that "fits" the company's past performance well. It builds on historical precedents and discernible trends to tell a cohesive, coherent, and credible story about where the company has been, and where it's headed.

- **Flexible and dynamic** – We touched on this earlier. A good model has a dynamic, adaptable architecture. For example, the model we'll build in this book employs a "modular" approach in which certain "supporting" schedules—the depreciation schedule, for instance—are built separately from the "core" financial statements that they support. (By "core" we mean the income statement, balance sheet, and statement of cash flows.) This modular approach makes the model dynamic. Why? Because any change to a supporting schedule—for instance, a switch from straight-line depreciation to an accelerated depreciation method on the depreciation schedule—will "flow through." It will automatically update any relevant line items that are on the core statements.

- **Easy to follow** – A good model simplifies the complex—yet without oversimplifying. Many enthusiastic modelers feel driven to come up with a big, complicated, detailed, robust recreation of a given company's business. Robustness is certainly a part of our goal, but true mastery lies in the modeler's ability to simplify where it would improve clarity, in order to communicate the story embodied in that recreation to an end user who isn't an expert, or who wasn't involved in building the model. Whether the end user is an internal manager or an external client, they should be able to follow the logic of your model's calculations, assumptions, and forecasts with enough clarity that they can use it on their own. A good model, in short, has an orderly progression—or "flow"—that is continuous, intuitive, and logical, and which makes it intelligible to many people, not just the person who built it. The power of a good model lies in its simplicity. Make your model no more complicated than it needs to be.

Vertical versus horizontal models

Vertical Models

Although there is no single correct way to lay out a model, two approaches are commonly used. One is to lay it out vertically. That means all the schedules are laid out on a single Excel worksheet.

Exhibit 2.1

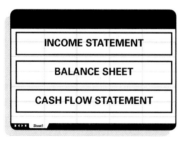

Compared to a horizontal layout, this layout confines you to one or a small number of worksheets and uses many more rows. There are advantages and downsides to this approach:

- **Advantage** – It's compact! You can have all of your analysis on one worksheet. This allows you to keep your focus in one area and in one view. A vertical layout is ideal for what's often called a "one pager" analysis or model. Example: An operating income model that forecasts from revenue to EBIT using mainly operating drivers. One can easily visualize keeping this analysis on a single worksheet. (A "one pager" is not always literally one page; it refers loosely to the fact that it's compact.)

- **Advantage** – It allows for easy alignment of columns and headings. A modeling best practice is, whenever possible, to keep the same column letters for the same projected years on different sheets or analyses. For example, you could make column K correspond to the first projected year on all the schedules. This would make it easier to audit cell references and to maintain consistency throughout the model.

- **Downside** – They can be tough to navigate. This is especially true if the model takes up many rows. But several Excel best practices exist that can help you navigate through a vertical model more quickly.

Horizontal Models

The second approach is to lay out your model horizontally.

Exhibit 2.2

In a horizontal model, each individual worksheet contains its own schedule and is linked to other schedules. The model we will create in this book is a horizontal one. This layout too has advantages and downsides:

- **Advantage** – Great readability! A horizontal model offers a cleaner, more intuitive layout. A user can readily access different schedules by simply reading the different tab labels.

- **Advantage** – It is easier to set up. To add functionality, you can simply insert new worksheets instead of building downward as you would in a vertical model.

- **Downside** – The model spreads out as worksheets are added, and too many sheets can begin to make it unwieldy and hard to navigate. But as with vertical models, there are Excel best practices that can help you navigate a horizontal model more quickly.

A Hybrid Layout

As we said, there's no universal best way to build a model. The question you should ask when constructing one is: What is it going to be used for? For example, the template we've created for your earnings model uses multiple supporting schedules. We could have opted for

a vertical model instead, but it probably would have been more cumbersome and less readable. What we could have done, however, is to create a hybrid model by combining elements of a horizontal layout and a vertical layout to suit our purposes Take a look at Exhibit 2.3:

Exhibit 2.3

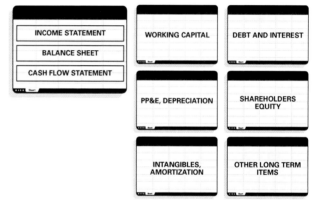

What are the strengths of this hybrid layout? In our opinion, it makes better sense to keep the core statements in a single (vertical) location. That way, you or a colleague can quickly scroll though income statement, balance sheet, and cash flow statement. But the supporting schedules are laid out horizontally, making them more readable and easier to access. There's no one correct way: The idea behind the hybrid is that you can mix and match the best parts of each, but let *purpose* be your over arching guide. What you're trying to do is to communicate, not stick to a rigid convention or a preconception of what's best.

 Please view the Online Companion for related supplementary media.

Cell comments

You can use **cell comments** to document or annotate a worksheet. Comments are like little digital Post-Its®. You can use them for many things: for example, to clarify some result or complexity within your model, leave a note or an instruction for another user, explain why you used a particular formula, or leave a general paper trail. When you insert a comment in a cell, Excel places a small red triangle in the upper right-hand corner of the cell to indicate that there is a comment in the cell (see Exhibit 2.5).

The model you will be working on uses comments extensively to source information from the financial statements, explain complexities, and highlight various concepts. Our models and templates are loaded with comments.

To view a comment, first switch on your Comment Indicator using the Office Button in Excel 2007 or File tab in Excel 2010/2013, Excel Options, Advanced menu:

✂ **Excel 2007:** 🄰🄻🅃 🄵 🄸 🄰 *(Alt F, I, A)*
✂ **Excel 2010/2013:** 🄰🄻🅃 🄵 🅃 🄰 *(Alt F, T, A)*

Exhibit 2.4

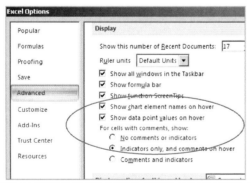

Excel 2007 environment displayed. Other versions of Excel will look slightly different.

Exhibit 2.5

A	B	C	D	E	F	G
1			**Comment Indicator**			
2						
3						Historical Ye
4						2005
5			**Ratios & Assumptions**			
6	x		Sales Growth			10.5%

To make the comment temporarily visible, hover your cursor over the cell (see Exhibit 2.6).

To view the comment without using the mouse, navigate to the cell using your arrow keys and then hold down ✂ **SHIFT + F2** *(Shift + F2)*.

To get out of comment viewing mode, hit the Esc key twice.

To insert a comment in a cell, use the same shortcut ✂ **SHIFT + F2** *(Shift + F2)*

Exhibit 2.6

A	B	C	D	E	F	G
1			**Comment Indicator**			
2						
3						Historical Ye
4						2005
5			**Ratios & Assumptions**			
6	x		Sales Growth			10.5%
7				**Training The Street:**		
8				Shift + F2 will let you read a		
9				cell comment. Hit ESC twice		
10				to exit the comment		
11						

Please view the Online Companion for related supplementary media.

2.2 WORKING WITH ASSUMPTIONS

Assumptions as drivers

The foundation of any financial model is its assumptions. Assumptions are the things you can change in a model to shape or drive your projections. This is why assumptions are also sometimes called **drivers**. An assumption is a kind of input that functions as a driver.

To make this notion clearer, let's examine the sales of a fictitious company, Trazeela Corp., forecasted by a sales growth rate driver. Let's assume that you've just used a model to project that Trazeela's sales will grow at a 10% rate next year. The formula in Excel for this would be:

Exhibit 2.7

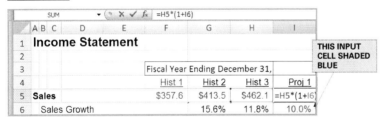

| Sales next projected year | = | Sales last year | x | (1 + 10% growth rate) |

Because assumptions are inputs, they are typically denoted in the color blue, as in the above example (more on using consistent color schemes later). Inputs are values or calculations that are entered directly into cells, or 'hard-coded,' and therefore do not reference or depend upon values or calculations in other cells. In this case, the 10% driver in cell I6 was is an input—it is an assumption being used to

drive the sales dollar amount in cell I5. Since it is an input, it can be changed. For example, if you thought Trazeela's sales growth would slow down even faster in Proj 1, then you could lower the growth rate to something smaller, like 5%.

Exhibit 2.8

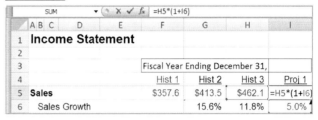

A model must have assumptions that are not only clear and well-defined but also credible and legitimate, because the integrity of the model depends heavily on the quality of your assumptions. Borrowing from the computer science community, practitioners refer to this as "Garbage In, Garbage Out". A model is only as good as the soundness of one's assumptions.

But before you even start thinking about your assumptions, you need to identify the correct drivers in the first place, because no matter how good your assumptions are, your results will be less defensible if you have the wrong driver. While there is certainly room for interpretation here, the "correct" drivers can be defined as the factors that best explain the direction (i.e., up or down) of certain key performance measures of the company's business (sales growth, for example).

The important exercise of choosing appropriate drivers points to a central challenge, and characteristic, of modeling: There are many different ways to forecast the same thing. To illustrate, here are of some key performance measures and their common drivers:

KEY PERFORMANCE MEASURE	COMMON DRIVER(S)
Sales	• Percent growth • Price x Volume • Market share x Market size • Industry specific measures: Sales per store or comp store sales growth in retail
Operating Expenses (COGS, SG&A, etc.)	• Margin based on sales • "Build-up" based on detailed numbers
Working Capital Items	• Days (based on sales or COGS, as appropriate) • Percent of sales or COGS
Capital Expenditures	• Percent of sales • Fixed dollar amount based on historical or expected levels • "Build-up" based on detailed numbers
Depreciation	• Percent of CapEx (vs. maintenance CapEx level), percent of net PP&E or percent of sales • Based on estimated useful lives of fixed assets and CapEx
Dividends	• Dividend payout ratio (based on net income) • Dividend per share • Fixed dollar amount based on historical or expected levels

KEY PERFORMANCE MEASURE	COMMON DRIVER(S)
Debt Repayment	• Known maturities of long-term debt instruments • "Sweep" with available free cash flow
Stock Buyback Program	• $ Repurchased: # of shares x estimated price per share (based on PE multiple) • # Repurchased: $ budgeted for repurchase/estimated price per share (based on PE multiple)
Other Key Items	• Taxes: Effective tax rate or marginal tax rate with adjustments to taxable income • Interest rates: Analysis of debt footnote or current market environment

In our sales example above, we projected Trazeela's sales using a growth driver approach. But what if we had reliable information about Trazeela's market share and the market size of its product? Then we may have been inclined to project sales using those metrics instead of a sales growth percentage. Or, what if we determined that Trazeela's sales were driven by industry-specific metrics? For example, Trazeela's retail performance might be driven by sales per store or comp store sales growth. Again, these metrics may serve as better drivers than a sales percentage growth driver. When we build our model together, we will dive further into forecasting concepts, making certain decisions along the way about how best to drive each performance measure. As we make these decisions for our sample company, remember that in the context of your real-world work, you should always customize your model for the particular company, industry, and circumstances you are modeling.

Entering exact figures

Here is another instance of the Garbage In, Garbage Out principle: the calculations generated by your financial model can never be more accurate than the numbers you put into it. To maximize the usefulness of the information you get from documents like 10-K filings, enter all numbers in full—exactly the way they appear in the document. Leave it to Excel to automatically round the numbers up or down. (What Excel will actually do depends on the format you selected: for example, currency, one decimal place, or with thousands separated by a comma).

Exhibit 2.9

	Enter as	Viewed as
Cash	25.382 ⟶	$25.4
Accounts Receivable, net	215.032 ⟶	215.0

Remember this principle: The fewer instructions you execute manually, and the more of them you just leave to Excel to automate, the less chance of error.

Here's an analogy you may be familiar with from Microsoft Word. Word automatically creates a line break when you reach the end of a line and keep typing. If you were an inexperienced user of Word and manually inserted your own line breaks instead, but then at some point changed the widths of your margins or the point size of your font,

the page would display incorrectly. It is better to allow Word to automatically reconfigure where the ends of your lines should be. The same is true for using tabs to make a paragraph indent, instead of manually clicking the space bar numerous times. The more you leave to Word—or Excel— to handle automatically, the fewer mistakes you'll make. These are powerful software programs with sophisticated machinery for handling automation. Take advantage of their built-in functionality!!

This principle is particularly true in the next topic we are about to explore.

Never input the same number twice!

Exhibit 2.10

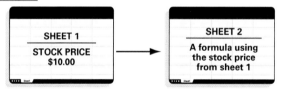

Example: On Sheet 1 you have a number—for instance, a company stock price. And on Sheet 2 you have a *formula* that uses that stock price.

You now need the stock price for a new formula you're building on a third sheet, Sheet 3. You feel tempted to type the same stock price again as an **input**, but you'd be wrong.

Exhibit 2.11

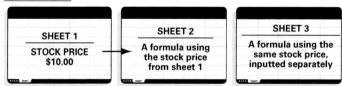

You would end up with **two** input cells that represent the same thing. Now, it may turn out that you'll remember to manually update the stock price in the two locations. But a colleague could well overlook the stock price in Sheet 3 and update only the first stock price—potentially creating a "domino effect" of subsequent miscalculations. What should you have done instead?

Reference all the stock prices back to the original input in Sheet 1. Efficient modelers never input the same number more than once.

Exhibit 2.12

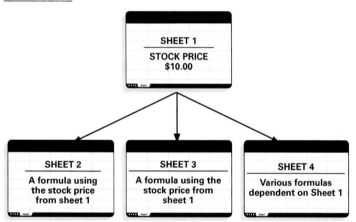

By letting just **one** cell input represent **one** item—even if that item is referenced in several places—you are allowing Excel to do what it does best: to flow automatically and make its own dynamic adjustments and recalculations as you move through your financial model building exercise. Such inputs are typically denoted in the color blue. (We'll say more about this in the paragraphs below.)

BEST PRACTICE

By letting Excel automate basic functions, and resisting the temptation to enter these functions manually yourself, you are letting the program do what it does best: Flow automatically and make its own dynamic adjustments and recalculations as you go along.

Meanwhile, keep this simple rule in mind when entering and referencing cell inputs in Excel: **Never input the same number twice.**

Breaking out inputs

Another **Best Practice** that lessens the chances of error is to break out inputs such as drivers separately and color-code them. In the example in Exhibit 2.13, we've assumed that Trazeela's sales revenue will grow 10% in the first projected year. So we've built a formula in cell I5 that uses our 10% assumption to calculate a dollar value for sales.

So far, so good. But let's say that, being inexperienced modelers, and knowing that calculations (or references on the same sheet) are typically denoted in **black** font—more on this below—we erroneously make this cell I5 **black**. Our math is correct, and for now it does happen to generate a valid number for sales in cell I5.

But what if a colleague wanted to change the 10% growth rate assumption to 11%? She would need to edit cell I5 directly—that is, manually—in order to change this figure. But the conventional color scheme that is used in modeling—inputs in blue, calculations in **black**—may lead them to miss the fact that a 10% input has been manually embedded—or hard-coded—into the formula. The result? Confusion.

 Please view the Online Companion for related supplementary media.

Exhibit 2.13

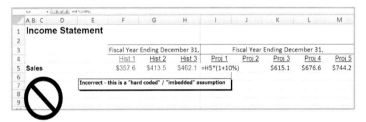

Instead, here's a good suggestion: Break out your drivers separately, and color-code them blue. This modeling **Best Practice** avoids confusion by intuitively communicating the model's logic to the next user who comes along after you.

Exhibit 2.14

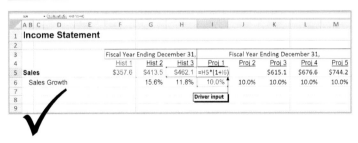

If your drivers are going to stay unchanged over time, you can use a modeling technique called **flatlining**. There will be many opportunities to practice flatlining as we build our

model together. For now, just recall that flatlining allows the user to change just one input cell and have that same driver carried forward into subsequent years.

Exhibit 2.15

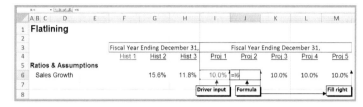

Using a consistent color scheme

All too often, Excel beginners make the mistake of using black font for every single cell in a model. But cells differ. Some contain a value, others a formula. Some cells drive the model, others contain a reference to a separate worksheet. As previous examples have shown, it's important to have something that helps you spot these differences quickly.

A color scheme is a great visual way to differentiate between cells. By instantly communicating each cell's content and purpose, a color scheme makes it easy for other users to follow the logic of your model.

The main thing is to be consistent. If you use green for references, use it throughout. That way, over time each color is automatically associated in your mind with a particular role or content. Here's a color scheme that we have found works well:

BLUE	=	inputs (historical values, assumptions, drivers).
BLACK	=	calculations and references on the same schedule/sheet.
GREEN	=	references from another schedule/sheet.
RED	=	warnings to another user or links to another model/file.

This is not a hard-and-fast color scheme, just one that we've found works well. You can adopt it or make up your own—unless your firm or team already has one that it uses. The key is consistency.

 Please view the Online Companion for related supplementary media.

Using consistent number formats

Using consistent number formats is another practice that helps to minimize confusion by better communicating the information in your model to the next user. Again, there's no hard-and-fast rule. You can adopt the formats we have suggested here, or create a set of your own if your firm or group doesn't already have Excel standards it uses. The model we'll be building together uses the following formats:

Number Type	Example of Suggested Format
Dollars in millions	$1,000.0
Numbers in millions	1,000.0
Percentages	10.0% (sometimes you will see 10.00%)
Multiples	15.6x
Per share statistics	$4.93 earnings per share or $0.25 dividend per share
Shares in millions	145.649

 Please view the Online Companion for related supplementary media.

2.3 WRITING BASIC FORMULAS

Historical ratios

Growth rates

So far, we've talked about the importance of developing sound assumptions and identifying the best drivers of important performance measures, such as sales. Historical ratios can provide an important framework to guide us in that process. Modelers calculate historical ratios, which indicate where a business has been, in order to get a sense of where the business is going. For example, a **historical growth rate** is a ratio describing the growth of some element of a business over some particular time period. The element is usually revenue, but it could be something else—number of units delivered, registered users, and so on. Analyzing growth rates, typically over three or more historical periods, can yield important insights about the direction of the business going forward. The formula for calculating a historical growth rate is:

$$\text{Historical growth rate} = \frac{\text{Change in the amount of an item since last year}}{\text{Last year's amount}}$$

For example:

$$\text{Sales growth rate} = \frac{(\text{This year's sales} - \text{Last year's sales})}{\text{Last year's sales}}$$

The historical growth rate concept itself is straightforward—the challenge is to translate it into a form we can use in Excel. To input the formula into Excel, you'll need to simplify the formula with a bit of algebra. The way to do this is to factor out "Last year's sales," The formula becomes:

$$\text{Sales growth rate} = \frac{\text{This year's sales}}{\text{Last year's sales}} - 1$$

Exhibit 2.16

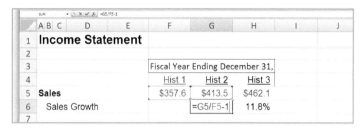

You now need to reference just two cells instead of three. It's efficiencies like this that make you a better modeler.

Margins

In the finance world, margins are informative indicators of a company's performance and current financial health. Commonly analyzed margins include the Gross Profit Margin, EBITDA margin, the EBIT margin, and the Net Income margin. Mathematically, a margin is defined as:

$$\text{Margin} = \frac{\text{Financial statistics}}{\text{Sales}}$$

A margin is therefore a kind of ratio. If a company's EBITDA margin is 25%, for example, that means it earns 25 cents in EBITDA for every $1 of sales.

A margin is a relative measure of profitability. A change in a margin over time helps you know if a company's profitability is improving or declining. Changes in margin therefore reflect the company's capacity to withstand a downturn and management's ability to maximize revenues and control expenses. In short, margins capture performance trends.

Exhibit 2.17

Please view the Online Companion for related supplementary media.

A B C	D	E	F	G	H	I	J	K
1	**Income Statement**							
2								
3			Fiscal Year Ending December 31,					
4			Hist 1	Hist 2	Hist 3			
5	**Sales**		$357.6	$413.5	$462.1			
7	EBITDA		$93.0	$99.2	$115.5			
9	*EBITDA Margin*		26.0%	24.0%	*=H7/H5*			

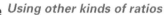

Using other kinds of ratios

In addition to analyzing margins, there are other historical performance ratios that can be helpful to examine when you're building a financial model. However, when you're modeling, you need to balance the benefit of calculating additional formulas against the time required to do so. That should tell you whether or not to go ahead with the calculation. There are four main kinds: **efficiency ratios**, **profitability ratios**, **liquidity ratios**, and **return ratios**.

The following is one example of a circumstance when it is helpful to go ahead and use an efficiency ratio:

Suppose you're forecasting a company's accounts receivable in future years. You might be tempted to think that, since accounts receivable is simply the balance owed from a credit sale, it must grow at the same rate as sales. Not necessarily. For instance, what if the company staff became more efficient in collecting its receivables? That would likely alter the accounts receivable relationship to sales. So you need to factor that in to be able to predict future accounts receivable accurately. By using an **efficiency ratio** that is

often referred to as 'receivable days,' you can measure the number of days it takes the company to collect receivables, in comparison to sales. This will give you a more accurate picture of what the future accounts receivable balance will be, because you are factoring in both sales growth and management's operating efficiency, which is a very useful level of detail. You will learn the formulas for efficiency ratios when we create the working capital schedule, and this will allow you to forecast both balance sheet and statement of cash flow items.

We have already briefly touched on **efficiency ratios**. **Profitability ratios** are just another name for margins. Here is a quick overview of the other two kinds:

• **Leverage ratios** – These ratios tell us about how a company is managing its funding, specifically, how it's using long-term debt. Practical uses of leverage ratios include measuring a company's debt-to-equity ratio, often called its "debt capacity," and measuring interest payments relative to debt balances, otherwise known as "affordability analysis." These ratios are necessary when examining a company's creditworthiness, much like an individual's credit score.

• **Return ratios** – These ratios measure the investment required to earn a profit. They help you understand how much a company is spending in order to make its earnings. Investors often use return ratios. Frequently, net income is compared to a company's equity balance to see what percentage of profits is being returned to equity investors.

Forecasting methods

There are different ways to forecast. To select a method, you need to understand what drives changes in the forecasted performance measure. In each case, it's important first to understand what makes that particular item increase or decrease and what else it may be correlated with, and only then choose a method for projecting it into the future.

Growth rates

Investors as well as job seekers are particularly keen on finding businesses that offer indications that they will be able to sell more goods or services this year than last year, because this points to growth and vitality. We can use a simple growth rate to forecast future sales. Suppose we think Trazeela Corp. can sell 6% more next year than last year's sales of $1 million. We simply take $1,000,000 and multiply it by (1+6%) to grow it by that expected 6%.

Margins

When you're analyzing data from previous years, it's also useful to quickly calculate margins to see what percentage of sales a company's costs are. For example, suppose the company's administrative costs have remained at approximately 15% of sales. Barring any major changes on the horizon or changes you've recently discovered, it should be safe to assume that administrative expenses as a percentage of sales will be similar. Multiply next year's expected sales of $1,060,000 by the assumed 15% to forecast administrative costs of $159,000.

Dollar amounts

You are quite likely to run into circumstances where you can't use a growth rate or a margin. Why? Many items in a company's financial statements can seem almost erratic in their behavior, which often makes forecasting difficult.

For instance, how do you project something that seems unrelated to sales and seems not to be growing or shrinking at a steady rate? An example would be a pension expense: It is not driven by sales revenue, and it fluctuates from year to year. In such cases, a good modeler often looks to an equity research report or management's disclosure in the financial statements to glean insights into the company's future performance, then projects that item as a dollar amount rather than using a growth rate or a margin.

2.4 SAFETY CHECKS

Stress testing

In financial modeling, an error made at one stage often carries over and builds into the next stage, creating a distorting effect that's cumulative. A *Best Practice* is to perform safety checks after you have built a formula in order to make sure your model is working correctly. This is called **stress testing**.

The first safety check is **Excel-based**: Have you created the right formula, and is it properly linked and copied? A second safety check involves **accounting**: Is your accounting correct, and is your forecasting behaving accordingly? Stress testing involves steps such as:

1. Increasing an assumption,
2. Decreasing the assumption,
3. Setting the assumption to zero, and
4. Flipping signs: turning a positive sign into a negative, or vice versa.

After each stress test we will observe its effect on the model and then ask: Does the result match what we expected? For example, increasing a sales growth rate should cause forecasted sales to rise. If it does, we can move on. If not, we need to find the source of the error and repair the model.

Auditing tools

As you can see, testing the model you're building will avoid errors. A model can have thousands of numbers, and it's easy to lose track of how they are all interconnected. Luckily, Excel gives you "auditing" tools that make it easy to trace your work and ensure the integrity of your model. Here are some of the most powerful auditing tools:

The F2 key The quickest way to see which other cells are included in a formula is to hit the F2 key. F2 activates Excel's "Edit Mode" and highlights any other number on the page that flows into the cell you have your cursor on. To exit from Edit Mode, just hit **Esc** key.

CTRL + **[** *(Control + [ )* Excel also lets you trace values that flow into a formula from a different sheet. When your cursor is on a cell that's equal to a cell on a separate sheet, you can hold down the Control key and press [to jump to the original source of the value. To return to the cell you were working on, press **F5** and then **Enter**. (Remember that F5 is Excel's "Go to" command.)

MODELING TIP: THE F2 KEY

Whenever you're working in an unfamiliar file, tread carefully because you don't know how all the cells are interconnected—in other words, whether and how some cells may affect others. So first thing, "walk around" the worksheet by using the "Edit Mode" (F2 key) to learn how the model was built. Get comfortable with its construction, and only then proceed.

The Auditing Toolbar – If you're working with a complex formula that has multiple references to other sheets as well as values on the same sheet, consider using Excel's auditing toolbar. Under the Formulas tab on the ribbon, select the Trace Precedents command (right above Trace Dependents). [ALT] [M] [P] *(Alt, M, P).* Trace Precedents draws blue arrows that show you which other cells affect the value of the cell you have selected. In other words, it reveals all the cells that flow into the formula you've selected. If there are references from another worksheet, a small icon will pop up. You can click on the dotted line and instantly go to the reference from another page. To access the auditing tools, go to the Formula tab [ALT] [M] *(Alt M)* as shown below.

Exhibit 2.18

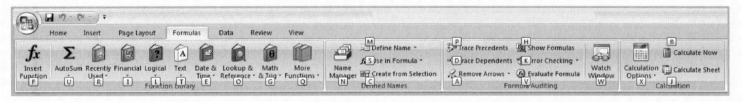

Now that we've discussed some basic modeling principles, it's time to dive in and "get smart" on the company you are about to build a model for. Getting smart means gathering all the relevant information we can find about the target company's industry and business. This will give us valuable insights into the trends, events, and other factors that affected the company's past performance and, more importantly, are likely to drive its future prospects.

This is a crucial step that inexperienced modelers often neglect in favor of a "plug n' chug" approach to modeling. Don't be tempted to take a shortcut here—it'll ultimately prove to be the long way around! Get smart. Taking a bit of time to familiarize yourself with the factors driving your target company's business will put you on the right foundation. Neglecting to do this will undercut your model's accuracy from the get-go.

3.1 TOP-DOWN ANALYSIS: KNOW YOUR TARGET COMPANY'S INDUSTRY

Before you focus on your target company's specific business and financials, the first thing to do to "get smart" is to build an understanding of its industry. This is commonly known as a "top down" approach to analysis. It means thinking through the high-level, external factors that can affect the company's performance. These broader industry factors may include:

- **Macroeconomic trends**

- **Shifts in consumer behavior or in corporate behavior**

- **Technological innovations**

- **Changes in the competitive landscape—for example, a wave of consolidations among the company's competitors**

- **New government policies and programs or new agency regulations**

- **Where in its lifecycle the industry is (particularly applies to cyclical industries)**

- **Secular trends driving the industry and how long they are likely to last**

This isn't an exhaustive list. There could be others. Before we undertake a top-down analysis, we first need to identify the company's industry so we can draw meaningful comparisons later on. At first glance this may look easy, but consider, for example, Apple Computer. Apple makes computers, right? So it seems to fit nicely in the **PC hardware industry**. But Apple also makes the software used in its computers. So is Apple in the computer hardware industry or the **software industry**, or both? Apple also makes the iPod, a category-defying, boundary-crossing product that, on its own, would tend to place the company in the **audio entertainment manufacturing industry**. Perhaps we might agree to tuck the iPad under the electronics hardware umbrella, but Apple is also a major distributor of digital music and video content through its iTunes platform. So is Apple a **media company** as well? Not to mention the iPhone, a **telecommunications industry product**.

Clearly, assigning a company to a particular industry can be a judgment call that's a little more art than science. This is increasingly true as modern, transnational companies expand into new markets and demographics to capture new growth opportunities. Although there are sometimes no right answers, there are tried-and-tested approaches experienced analysts use to place a company's operations in one industry or another. These approaches include:

• **Revenues (or sales)** – Modelers analyze the proportion of revenues generated by a company's different business lines to compare its embeddedness in one industry rather than another. Take the example of a fictitious company, Krabbator Ltd: 95% of Krabbator's revenue comes from the tractors it makes and sells. The remaining 5% of its revenue comes from its financing arm, which loans money to farmers to fund big-ticket purchases. Clearly, Krabbator is primarily a tractor company, not a financing group. It belongs to the farming machinery industry or, more broadly, the heavy equipment industry.

• **Production** – Analysts also examine a company's production processes to categorize it. Going back to our tractor example, it may make sense to place a company like Krabbator, which *designs and manufactures* entire tractors, in a different sub-industry than a company that makes *tractor spare parts*, or one that *assembles* tractor parts into a finished product. For the same reason, Seagate and Western Digital, which make computer hard drives, belong in a different sub-industry than Dell and HP, which make computers.

• **Databases** – There are several database resources you can consult to get help, to get you started, or to crosscheck your analysis. Business classification systems, such as the North American Industry Classification System (NAICS), were created to enable better comparability between businesses in the US and in its North American neighbors. These systems have very comprehensive databases. The downside is that they can be outdated or too broad and can be cumbersome to navigate.

• **Other resources** – Company disclosures such as 10-K filings and research reports can be excellent resources, but be careful always to consider the source and to filter out potential pro-company biases in these documents. Again, let's look at a tractor example: Imagine you are analyzing a small company that is preparing to go public. The company primarily makes seat cushions for tractors and other vehicles. Its IPO prospectus displays an impressive list of competitors, including leading tractor makers like John Deere. Clearly, the business model of a company like Deere, and the industry factors that affect its performance, are likely to differ markedly from those of a seat cushion manufacturer. And yet the company in our example may have its own motives for listing Deere as a competitor. After all, the IPO prospectus is essentially a marketing document for prospective investors.

As modelers, we must remember that our primary goal in doing a top-down analysis is to determine the external factors that genuinely affect our target company's performance.

3.2 KNOW YOUR COMPANY

A frequently asked question: *"Do I need to know everything about a company in order to build a model? Just how do professionals build models in a few hours when they have all of this information to absorb?"*

We will let you in on a little secret… You don't have to know everything about a company to get a model up and running. Sure, if you had the time, it would be great to read everything you could about the company. But as in all things, you must exercise balance and discretion and apportion your energies appropriately.

To gather enough data to build a model without going overboard, here's our suggested approach:

1. Review the latest company filings. We typically use the 10-K, annual report, or 20-F. These documents typically contain a description of the business and discuss important issues such the company's competition, its products, and risk factors. We've provided you with the 10-K.

2. Read through **TTS's pre-modeling questions**.

You can download this through the Online Companion, and it is part of the provided Case Study.

3. a) Think of these questions as a checklist to guide you as you search for relevant information in the filings. Some of the questions are designed to get you to think about the company's history. Other questions lead to direct inputs in the model.

   b) Our pre-modeling questions are a great tool you can use to analyze other companies as well.

4. Gain access to an equity research report. This may be subscription-based, or your firm may have a license.

   a) Recent reports will bring you up to speed on current events and analyses.

   b) One of the best reports you can use is an **initiating coverage report** or a **launching coverage** report. (It may go by some other similar name, depending on the analyst or bank.) This is the research report analysts write when they begin covering a company. It typically provides comprehensive analysis and useful background information about the company and its industry.

5. Visit the company's website, especially its Investor Relations and its Recent News & Events pages.

6. Finally, a number of subscription-based database services and public websites provide company analysis.

These sources should be enough to get you started on building a good, defensible model. If you plan on doing a thorough analysis, however, we strongly suggest that you acquire as much information about your company as possible. For example, you may want to undertake your own proprietary research on the company and its industry or read investor call transcripts.

 Please view the Online Companion for related supplementary media.

Navigating the 10-K

For the company around which we'll be building a financial model, we'll use a 10-K or annual report to gather most of the information we'll need. But a 10-K isn't something you can just launch into. Although the level of detail in a typical 10-K makes it a very useful document for modelers, its substantial size and factual density are intimidating to beginners and can slow down even savvy modelers. You need a plan of attack, a navigation method of that allows you to extract useful details from it without becoming bogged down and overwhelmed. We're about to give you one.

As you gain experience using 10-K filings, you will naturally develop your own strategic approach. Meanwhile, you can use our "10-K Sherpa Guide" to help you navigate your way up the learning slopes of this challenging report.

The 10-K Sherpa Guide: What's where
The first thing to note is that a 10-K has three sections you will find particularly relevant as a modeler:

• **The Management's Discussion & Analysis (MD&A)**

• **Financial Statements (income statement, balance sheet and cash flow)**

• **Financial Footnotes**

Where you'll find these sections in a 10-K may vary from company to company and even filing to filing. But typically, they appear one after another and in the order in which we've listed them above.

Don't be turned off by the dry accounting language and technical verbiage. Our 10-K Sherpa Guide will show you how to extract specific information from the document.

The Three Biggies
Let's briefly look at all three primary sections, starting with the **financial statements**, which contain what's often referred to as the **core statements** — the Income Statement, Balance Sheet, and Statement of Cash Flows. To become an efficient modeler, you need to know where to find these. But once you do, you will still need some explanations of trends and future assumptions. That's why you need to become familiar with a few other major sections of a 10-K, such as the **MD&A**.

MODELING TIP

The absolute first thing to do when you open a 10-K is to turn to the Income Statement. It's usually about halfway through the document. Bookmark this page with a dog-ear. It will now serve as your Reference Point. Now every time you pick up this 10-K, you'll know right away that the MD&A section immediately precedes your Reference Point, and the Financial Footnotes immediately follow it.

The MD&A is one of the most important sections of a 10-K and a rich source of information. It concisely compares the current period to the last, offers management's view of the next year, and highlights any major events that occurred in the past 12 months or are expected in the future.

Management often provides a highly useful qualitative, and even sometimes quantitative, outlook for upcoming years. This may help you determine your future growth rates and margins.

Finally, the **footnotes** following the financial statements provide details for understanding the accounting of the items on the "core statements"—specifically, the company's income, expenses and balances. In the footnotes, you find things such as the expected debt repayment schedule for the next five years, the difference between the federal tax rate and the company's effective tax rate, and the breakdown of definite life and indefinite life intangibles. Think of core financial statements as a summary, and the footnotes as all the supporting detail.

Here are some key items commonly discussed in the financial footnotes:

- **Accounting policies**
- **Non-recurring items**
- **Property, plant and equipment**
- **Debt and operating leases**
- **Breakdown of other income / expense**

- **Taxes (special items and tax rates)**
- **Employee and pension programs**
- **Overview of quarterly financials**
- **Segment and/or geographic detail**
- **Equity: option and share repurchase programs**

Here is a sample 10-K layout to help you become familiar with where to look to find the information you need. We have highlighted in grey the two items (numbers 7 and 8) that contain the MD&A, financial statements, and financial footnotes.

Exhibit 3.1

SCHEMATIC LAYOUT OF A 10-K

Item 1	Business description
Item 2	Properties
Item 3	Legal proceedings
Item 4	Submission of matters to a vote of security holders
Item 5	Market for registrant's common stock and related shareholder matters
Item 6	Selected financial data (typically, 5 or more years)
Item 7	Management's Discussion & Analysis of financial condition and results of operations
Item 8	Financial statements and supplementary data (footnotes)
Item 9	Changes in and disagreements with accountants on accounting and financial disclosure
Item 10	Directors and executive officers*
Item 11	Executive compensation*
Item 12	Security ownership of certain beneficial owners (5% or more) and management*
Item 13	Certain relationships and related transactions*
Item 14	Principal Accountant Fees and Services*
Item 15	Exhibits, Financial Statement Schedules and Reports on Form 8-K

*These five astericked items are often incorporated by reference in the company's proxy statement, which is typically filed around the same time as the 10-K.

Risk factors – In the MD&A section, pay special attention to the discussion of risk factors. Essentially, each risk factor represents a potential near-term or long-term "challenge" the company faces. You can therefore ask: Based on what I know about this company's strengths and weaknesses, how do I expect it to handle this challenge going forward? Is the company well-positioned to respond to this challenge?

If the answer is yes, then the risk factor can actually be an opportunity for the company to improve its performance. Your assumptions should, in turn, reflect this positive outlook by, for example, increasing sales growth or margin expansion. By contrast, if you believe the company will face great difficulty in mitigating one or more of these risks, then your assumptions should reflect this more pessimistic outlook in the form of declining sales growth or margin contraction.

 Please view the Online Companion for related supplementary media.

Beyond the 10-K

As a modeler, there are other important complementary resources you can use not only to bolster but also to double-check the information available in a company's annual 10-K (and in their quarterly 10-Q) filings. These include:

• **Company press releases, presentations, and conference calls** – Outside their formal 10-K filings with the SEC, many companies communicate with investors and analysts in other less formal ways. These informal disclosures can be invaluable sources of information that help you fill in the blanks by offering insights into the company's internal strategy and expectations. Expect, however, to find a natural 'marketing' bias in them. Management has reasons to present the company's performance in the best light possible.

• **Research reports** – Research reports can be a rich source of insights into company performance. As with company disclosures, be vigilant in spotting and sorting out any potential pro-company bias of the research analysts. They are paid to develop investment opinions that conclude with a "buy" or "sell" recommendation on the stocks of companies within their assigned universe.

The analysis and commentary that make up a research report are designed to fit into an overall investment theme or "story" that the analyst has crafted around the company's stock. Although these reports can be sound, well-researched, and based on very reasonable and robust analysis, expert modelers developing an opinion about a company's performance rely first on publicly available information about it. Only then does the modeler consult research reports to cross-check or double-check her assumptions. In summary, research reports can be excellent secondary resources.

3.3 CHOOSING ASSUMPTIONS

Identifying growth, revenue, and expense drivers is half the battle. The other half is actually choosing the assumptions that underlie and help you to put numerical values to those drivers!

To make sound assumptions, you need to know the underlying business and industry. The past is always a useful guide and a starting point. But to get a sense of the past, you must feel comfortable navigating through financial documents. Some modelers even rely on statistical tools such as averages and medians to guide them. But be careful not to rely mechanically on a technique without carefully considering what will happen in the future.

For example, what if we used the average of the past three years' sales growth rates to drive future sales? Do we really believe that next year's sales and projected years' sales from here on out will grow at a rate equal to the average of the past three years? Your technique will signal your expectations about the future.

If your information and analyses lead you to expect changes in the company's future performance, you'll need to make adjustments. These could reflect revised management expectations, variance in equity research opinions, or a change in market conditions.

In any case, make sure ultimately that your assumptions are reasonable, meaning they should be able to pass the "smell test" of common sense. They should also be defensible in the sense that you can explain to a colleague where you got them by sourcing them back to specific financial statements, management guidance, or research.

Let's Start Modeling...

Imagine you are building a house from the ground up and are responsible for all aspects of construction. You can't just start to build without a blueprint. You'll need to look at the project on what we might call a "macro" and a "micro" level. The "macro" level involves conceiving the structure and layout of the entire building, and drawing floor plans from an architectural standpoint. Once you have the structure and floor plans laid out, then you can tackle the "micro" level. This involves designing the layout of specific rooms and figuring out the best way to put in the plumbing, ventilation systems, dry wall, and electrical wiring. Even after this, you still can't just go in and start building. In all aspects of the home building, there are building codes, architectural standards, and engineering best practices that you'll need to familiarize yourself with and follow. You'll also discover that, although all construction companies follow roughly the same sequence of steps, there is some room for discretionary choice. Each group of practitioners brings their own set of approaches and styles.

Financial model construction is somewhat like building a house. As you build this model, a discernible pattern will emerge on both a "macro" and a "micro" level. The macro level reflects the particular sequence in which we create our core statements and supporting schedules. We begin by setting up the core statements. Next, we look at the company's internal sources for funding growth (working capital, property, plant & equipment, intangibles, and other long-term assets and liabilities). Finally, we schedule the company's external funding from equity and debt holders. This is like creating the rooms in a home. And yet within each room, there is a specific layout of where things should go and in what order. This is the "micro" level of model building.

The key thing to keep in mind is that the end result is mostly the same across practitioners: most earnings models are similar, but how they are built reflects the personal style of the modeler, and the needs of the end user.

I. "Macro" Level: Modular Approach

In this course, we'll use a **modular approach** to construct our earnings model. This means that many items on our core statements (i.e., the income statement, balance sheet, and cash flow statement) will be forecasted using information contained on 'supporting' schedules (see Exhibit 4.1).

Exhibit 4.1

Core Statements

Supporting Statements

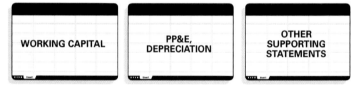

We are deciding to build this model horizontally, meaning that we will build these supporting schedules on separate Excel worksheets. That way, they can do most of the 'dirty work' for our core statements (i.e., forecasting) while serving as conduits of information between the core statements. The other benefit of the horizontal model is that we can keep it organized and visually navigable.

The core statements will be the first three worksheets with resulting supporting schedule sheets added to the right. Because of the critical role these supporting schedules play, it is important to properly link our worksheets together.

Note that this type of model can also be built vertically if you prefer. Again, there is no set way to create a model.

 Please view the Online Companion for related summary media.

II. "Micro" Level: Pattern of Forecasting

Now that the model is laid out from a macro perspective, we are ready to discuss an approach for laying out a specific worksheet or schedule. The micro level reflects a particular sequence <u>within</u> each schedule, which we'll refer to as our **pattern of forecasting**. This pattern includes the following steps:

1. Reference any relevant relationship drivers
2. Enter (or reference) historical content
3. Analyze historical content
4. Choose and forecast drivers
5. Project dollar amounts from these drivers
6. Link forecasted items to the core statements

Step One requires establishing relationship driver(s) used to forecast certain key items on the schedule. For example, sales could be referenced from the income statement to help drive accounts receivable projections on the working capital schedule. We will cover relationship drivers in more detail when we reach the working capital schedule.

Step Two involves entering a company's historical information taken from a company filing or other source such as a press release. For some schedules, the required historical information has been previously entered in another schedule; in such cases, we can simply reference— in other words, build links to—the relevant line items. This is consistent with our rule about minimizing inputs. Remember: the less blue, the better.

Step Three The reason for entering (or referencing) the historical information is to prepare our model for this next step, which is to analyze the historical content. This step involves a fair degree of subjective analysis (or "eyeballing") as well as objective analysis. By eyeballing, we mean undertaking a quick general overview of the numbers and drawing some subjective conclusions. This can allow us to develop some cursory insights into what's happening with the target company.

The more objective analytics involve a variety of calculations. Recall our earlier discussion of growth rates and margins. Upon calculating these statistics for our target company, do you notice any trends? Would it make sense at this point to calculate additional statistical measures such as averages, medians, or best-fit lines? Are the most recent data likely to remain roughly the same in the future?

Step Four Once you have an initial sense of where the company has been, you are better prepared to pick reasonable drivers. This step involves mechanically building drivers (for example, flatlines), ensuring that these inputs are color-coded blue to help the next user locate them. After the drivers are mechanically built, enter in a reasonable assumption that you can work with for the time being. We recommend that you do not spend too much time agonizing over any one driver at this point. Wait instead until the model is complete; then you can look at the whole picture and refine your drivers into their final form.

Step Five Once you have the drivers in place, the next thing to do is to project dollar amounts based on those drivers. This is the toughest step because you have to perform a little algebraic manipulation of our previous formulas. For example, let's examine the relationship of a growth rate between two years.

Old formula for historical analysis:

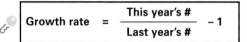

$$\text{Growth rate} = \frac{\text{This year's \#}}{\text{Last year's \#}} - 1$$

Historically, we were solving for a growth rate. But in Step Four, above, you specified what the future growth rate was going to be. So you are no longer solving for the growth rate but rather for this year's #.

We then rewrite the growth rate relationship to solve for a projected dollar amount:

New formula for projecting a dollar amount:

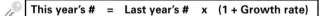

$$\text{This year's \#} = \text{Last year's \#} \times (1 + \text{Growth rate})$$

The new formula makes intuitive sense. If we are planning to grow a number, we would reference last year's number and multiply it by one plus the growth date driver.

Step five can get tricky if you have more complicated relationships but the general idea is the same. We will encounter more complicated relationships when we get to the working capital schedule.

Step Six involves linking key items back to the core statements. There is one final point about the pattern of forecasting. Let's revisit the analogy of laying out a room in a home. A typical room has specific locations for it components. For instance, the walls are always on the sides. The floor is, well, at the bottom. The electrical outlets are embedded in the walls or floors. In short, even though the rooms may vary, they share some basic elements of layout.

The same can be said for schedules. The first five of the six steps of the pattern of forecasting have specific locations on a spreadsheet. Here are they are again:

1. Reference any relevant relationship drivers
2. Enter (or reference) historical content
3. Analyze historical content
4. Choose and forecast drivers
5. Project dollar amounts from these drivers

These five items are represented visually below:

Exhibit 4.2

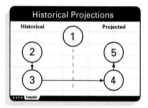

Not all schedules look like this, but see if you can spot patterns. We will cover this sequence at the beginning of every schedule with an overview of what is to come.

Please view the Online Companion for related summary media.

Flow-of-funds

As we build the model, we'll utilize a **flow-of-funds** concept to trace the connections between core statements and schedules. The flow-of-funds is especially helpful to visual learners, because it allows them to grasp the big picture of the model's layout as we are building it piece by piece.

The other purpose is to help illustrate the relationships between the different schedules and what direction the cash flows, dollar amounts, drivers and other numbers are moving between schedules. For example, the income statement and cash flow statement are related to each other. Here is the initial set up:

Exhibit 4.3

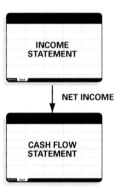

We know that the income statement and the cash flow statement are connected by net income. The net income is referenced from the income statement and flows to the cash flow statement. So the flow-of-funds would show the relationship in this way:

Exhibit 4.4

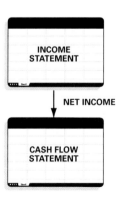

As we start to add more schedules and have more complex relationships, we will continue to draw lines in the flow-of-funds diagram to keep track of these relationships. Here is a sample of flow-of-funds after the working capital and depreciation schedule have been completed.

Exhibit 4.5

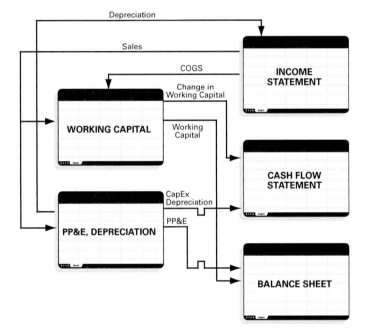

The flow-of-funds can be a useful visual cue for helping cement new understandings, especially as we progress toward more complex stages of the model. As we complete each section, we will use the flow-of-funds to generate a 'big picture' understanding of what has happened.

A third purpose of the flow-of-funds is to illustrate the overall the sequence of modeling. This may be a hard concept to grasp initially, but don't be overly concerned: We will lay out the foundation. There is no single path to the finish line. Modelers have different ways to build an earnings model. The thing to remember is that our overall sequence is non-linear. For example, on the income statement, you can't just start at the top with sales and model, in a direct and linear way, to net income and earnings per share. Why not?

Well, you will find that there are various points of the model where you can't move forward because you need either a schedule, another number, or another driver. When you start from the top down and try to forecast the income statement, you end up getting stuck at depreciation expense. You will be forced to pause, move away from the income statement, and build a depreciation forecast schedule.

On that schedule you will be responsible for forecasting capital expenditure assumptions and depreciation expense assumptions.

Once that schedule is completed, you can then reference the depreciation expense number back to the income statement and move on. We call these various points in the model **stuck points** to remind ourselves to build a new schedule, or forecast (or link in) another component to get past the stuck point. A primary takeaway from all this is that the model is not built in a linear fashion. As an exercise, see if you can identify the various stuck points in the model as we are going through the steps.

Because this sequencing issue can be tricky, we have developed a specific pattern and order to our teaching methodology. The following is an annotated guide to building a financial model essentially from scratch. Although you may be tempted to skip ahead or just build parts of the model on your own, we strongly suggest that you trust our time-tested method and follow the annotated steps. Remember: Although there is no single best way when it comes to details, there is a pattern when it comes to basic principles. We are ready to begin!

Please view the Online Companion for related supplementary media.

4.1 THE CORE STATEMENTS

The purpose of this section is to get the core statements up and running. We'll start by setting up the various line items for the core statements. We will then input historical information for the income statement and balance sheet. Next, we'll analyze the historical information to help us make the assumptions that will drive our projections.

Typically, guidelines for formatting vary across professions and organizations, and with individual preferences. This course pack adheres to a generic style of formatting that one might expect to see at a typical financial services company. Please stick rigidly with this style only while you're building your training model. Once you've learned how, you should then seek your organization's guidance when making formatting decisions (see Exhibit 4.6 on right).

Exhibit 4.6

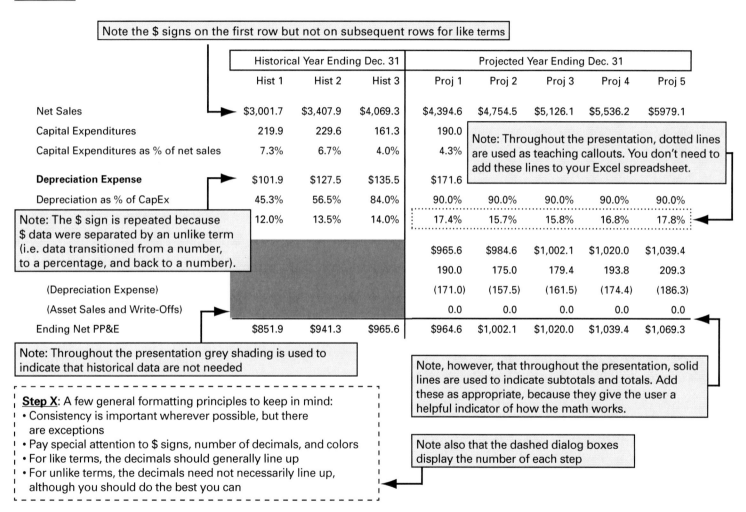

Note the $ signs on the first row but not on subsequent rows for like terms

	Historical Year Ending Dec. 31			Projected Year Ending Dec. 31				
	Hist 1	Hist 2	Hist 3	Proj 1	Proj 2	Proj 3	Proj 4	Proj 5
Net Sales	$3,001.7	$3,407.9	$4,069.3	$4,394.6	$4,754.5	$5,126.1	$5,536.2	$5979.1
Capital Expenditures	219.9	229.6	161.3	190.0				
Capital Expenditures as % of net sales	7.3%	6.7%	4.0%	4.3%				
Depreciation Expense	$101.9	$127.5	$135.5	$171.6				
Depreciation as % of CapEx	45.3%	56.5%	84.0%	90.0%	90.0%	90.0%	90.0%	90.0%
	12.0%	13.5%	14.0%	17.4%	15.7%	15.8%	16.8%	17.8%
				$965.6	$984.6	$1,002.1	$1,020.0	$1,039.4
				190.0	175.0	179.4	193.8	209.3
(Depreciation Expense)				(171.0)	(157.5)	(161.5)	(174.4)	(186.3)
(Asset Sales and Write-Offs)				0.0	0.0	0.0	0.0	0.0
Ending Net PP&E	$851.9	$941.3	$965.6	$964.6	$1,002.1	$1,020.0	$1,039.4	$1,069.3

Note: Throughout the presentation, dotted lines are used as teaching callouts. You don't need to add these lines to your Excel spreadsheet.

Note: The $ sign is repeated because $ data were separated by an unlike term (i.e. data transitioned from a number, to a percentage, and back to a number).

Note: Throughout the presentation grey shading is used to indicate that historical data are not needed

Step X: A few general formatting principles to keep in mind:
- Consistency is important wherever possible, but there are exceptions
- Pay special attention to $ signs, number of decimals, and colors
- For like terms, the decimals should generally line up
- For unlike terms, the decimals need not necessarily line up, although you should do the best you can

Note, however, that throughout the presentation, solid lines are used to indicate subtotals and totals. Add these as appropriate, because they give the user a helpful indicator of how the math works.

Note also that the dashed dialog boxes display the number of each step

STEP 1

Set up the income statement

Use company filings, company-provided financial reports, or research reports to provide the appropriate line items.

Add more detail if it helps you to analyze the company's financials, but try to keep the layout as simple and clear as possible.

Add the appropriate ratios and financial metrics for the company's given industry, as applicable.

The following is an example of a typical template, but feel free to customize/it for the particular circumstances of your work.

It is common to consolidate line items such as SG&A (selling, general & administrative) expenses.

If a breakout of interest expense/income is available, you should provide that detail using two separate lines. On the income statement, the company will usually give you "interest expense, net"—that is, interest expense minus interest income. You will then have to search the footnotes for a more detailed breakout.

Notice that we're calculating diluted EPS (net income divided by diluted shares outstanding) and not basic EPS (net income divided by basic shares outstanding). This helps to keep our layout clear and easy to follow. Also, when analyzing a company, investors typically focus more on diluted EPS. (For more information on the difference between diluted shares outstanding and basic shares outstanding, please refer to TTS's Corporate Valuation Self-Study Package.)

REFER TO SCREENSHOT ON THE RIGHT ⟶

 Please view the Online Companion for related supplementary media.

Income Statement for TTS Sample Company

Dollars in millions, except per share data

	Fiscal Year Ending December 31,			Fiscal Year Ending December 31,					5 Year CAGR
	Hist 1	Hist 2	Hist 3	Proj 1	Proj 2	Proj 3	Proj 4	Proj 5	
Sales									
Cost of goods sold, excluding depreciation (1)									
Gross profit									
SG&A expenses, excluding amortization									
Other operating (income) / expenses									
EBITDA									
Depreciation (1)									
Amortization									
EBIT (2)									
Interest expense									
Interest (income)									
Other non-operating (income) / expense									
Pretax income									
Income taxes (3)									
Net income (4)									
Diluted weighted average shares in millions									
Earnings per share									
Ratios & assumptions									
Sales growth rate									
Gross margin									
SG&A expenses (as a % of sales)									
Other operating (income) / expenses ($ amount)									
Other non-operating (income) / expense ($ amount)									
Effective tax rate									

NOTES

....

....

....

....

STEP 2

Set up the balance sheet

NOTES

Balance Sheet for TTS Sample Company

Dollars in millions, except per share data

	Fiscal Year Ending December 31,			Fiscal Year Ending December 31,				
	Hist 1	Hist 2	Hist 3	Proj 1	Proj 2	Proj 3	Proj 4	Proj 5
Cash								
Accounts receivable, net								
Inventories								
Other current assets								
Total current assets								
PP&E, net								
Definite life intangibles								
Indefinite life intangibles								
Goodwill								
Other long-term assets								
Total assets								
Accounts payable								
Accrued liabilities								
Other current liabilities								
Total current liabilities								
Revolver								
Long-term debt								
Deferred income taxes								
Other long-term liabilities								
Total liabilities								
Total equity								
Total liabilities and equity								
Parity check (A=L+E)								

Use company filings, company-provided financial reports, or research reports to determine the appropriate line items.

Use simplifications or a more detailed breakout of line items as appropriate. Base your decision on how you intend to project these items in future periods.

In general, intangibles should be broken out into three categories: (1) **goodwill**, (2) **definite life intangibles**, and (3) **indefinite life intangibles**. We'll discuss this in more detail on the amortization and other long-term items schedules. For now, suffice it to say that we break these items out because they are projected differently. As always, you will want to search the financial footnotes for greater detail on these items.

You will also notice that, in our suggested layout, there is no debt listed under current liabilities. Instead, you should model debt separately using two categories: (1) **long-term debt**, which includes interest bearing liabilities with maturities that are greater than one year; and (2) the **revolver**, which includes interest-bearing liabilities with maturities that are less than one year.

To simplify, consider adding the current portion of long term-debt to the long-term debt category. Also, again to simplify, consider placing only the revolving credit facility in the revolver line item and moving all other types of debt to long-term.

The following is an example of a typical template, but feel free to customize it for your particular work circumstances.

 Please view the Online Companion for related supplementary media.

Cash Flow Statement for TTS Sample Company

Dollars in millions, except per share data

	Fiscal Year Ending December 31,				
	Proj 1	Proj 2	Proj 3	Proj 4	Proj 5
Operating activities					
Net income					
Stock-based compensation expense					
Depreciation					
Amortization					
(Increase) / decrease in working capital					
Change in other long-term assets and liabilities					
Cash flow from operating activities					
Investing activities					
Capital expenditures					
Additions to definite life intangibles					
Cash flow from investing activities					
Cash flow available for financing activities					
Financing activities					
Issuance / (repayment) of revolver					
Issuance of long-term debt					
(Repayment) of long-term debt					
Repurchase of equity					
Dividends					
Option proceeds					
Cash flow from financing activities					
Net change in cash					
Beginning cash balance					
Ending cash balance					

Use company filings, company-provided financial reports, or research reports to determine the appropriate line items.

Historical data are not needed on this schedule because they are often difficult to reconcile precisely with the income statement and balance sheet. Historical data can be included for comparative purposes.

Ensure that this sheet is set up in a format consistent with the income statement and balance sheet. Projected years should appear in the same columns across each of the core statements (for example, column L is used for the same year on the IS, BS, and CF statement). This will make it easier to check for errors as we go along and to audit the model once it is finished.

 Please view the Online Companion for related supplementary media.

Use company filings or company-provided financial reports to input the historical income statement data. Form 10-K filings and annual reports provide historical annual data.

Adjust and normalize the historical data for any non-recurring/unusual items. *This step has already been completed for you in the template. For more information on normalizing, please refer to our Corporate Valuation Self-Study Package.*

Be sure to <u>exclude</u> depreciation and amortization from the historical operating expenses.

- **Depreciation** expense is usually 'buried' in COGS – it is not typically broken out separately on the company's income statement. It can usually be found on the cash flow statement or in a financial footnote describing the company's Property, Plant & Equipment (PP&E).

- **Amortization** expense is typically 'buried' in SG&A. It can usually be found on the cash flow statement or in a financial footnote describing the company's intangible assets.

Calculate the historical ratios, appropriate growth rates, and effective tax rate.

- Margins are calculated by dividing a particular item by sales. For example:

$$\text{Gross Margin} = \frac{\text{Gross profit}}{\text{Sales}}$$

- Growth rates are calculated by dividing current period's value by the previous period's value, and subtracting one:

$$\text{Growth Rates} = \frac{\text{Current Period's value}}{\text{Previous period's value}} - 1$$

- The effective tax rate is calculated by dividing income taxes by the company's pre-tax income:

$$\text{Effective Tax Rate} = \frac{\text{Income taxes}}{\text{Pre-tax income}}$$

Note: The calculated effective tax rate may be different than the effective tax rate disclosed by the company. That's because historical inputs have been normalized for non-recurring items.

REFER TO SCREENSHOT ON THE RIGHT ⟶

 Please view the Online Companion for related supplementary media.

	Fiscal Year Ending December 31,			Fiscal Year Ending December 31,					5 Year CAGR
	Hist 1	Hist 2	Hist 3	Proj 1	Proj 2	Proj 3	Proj 4	Proj 5	
Sales $\qquad$ Inputs are BLUE! →	$4,172.6	$4,429.2	$4,836.0						
Cost of goods sold, excluding depreciation (1)	2,383.7	2,509.2	2,764.7						
Gross profit	1,788.9	1,920.0	2,071.2 ◄						
SG&A expenses, excluding amortization	819.5	848.7	895.1						
Other operating (income) / expenses	0.0	0.0	0.0						
EBITDA	969.4	1,071.4	1,176.1 ◄						
Depreciation (1)	158.9	171.2	178.3						
Amortization	21.6	18.4	17.9						
EBIT (2)	788.8	881.7	979.9 ◄						
Interest expense	65.3	67.9	89.5						
Interest (income)	(1.7)	(1.4)	(1.5)						
Other non-operating (income) / expense	0.0	0.0	0.0						
Pretax income	725.3	815.2	891.9 ◄						
Income taxes (3)	266.2	298.4	324.7						
Net income (4)	**$459.1**	**$516.8**	**$567.3** ◄						
Diluted weighted average shares in millions	264.532	256.934	248.292						
Earnings per share	**$1.74**	**$2.01**	**$2.28** ◄						

Calculations (**BLACK**) Formulas

Ratios & assumptions

Sales growth rate		6.2%	9.2%	
Gross margin	42.9%	43.3%	42.8%	
SG&A expenses (as a % of sales)	19.6%	19.2%	18.5%	
Other operating (income) / expenses ($ amount)	$0.0	$0.0	$0.0	
Other non-operating (income) / expense ($ amount)	0.0	0.0	0.0	
Effective tax rate	36.7%	36.6%	36.4%	

Calculations: Tip
Use custom number format
to align parentheses
0.0%_);(0.0%)

1) Hist 1 and Hist 3 cost of goods sold adjusted for Business Realignment Initiatives of $2.119 million and $22.459 million respectively.

2) Depreciation excludes costs of $21.8 million in Hist 3, representing accelerated depreciation in cost of products sold on assets taken out of service.

3) Hist 3 taxes have been adjusted $44.375 related to the pre-tax $119.0 million of business realignment charges.

4) Hist 3 results have been adjusted to exclude $119.0 million pre-tax of business realignment charges.

NOTES

Use historical data, research reports, or management guidance to help determine appropriate assumption drivers.

– As a helpful guide, ask yourself: Are the assumptions I've chosen reasonable and defensible?

Choose an appropriate method for forecasting sales. Keep in mind that drivers are company—and industry—specific. Drivers can be detailed or simple, depending on the purpose of your model:

– **Detailed drivers**: These can provide a greater degree of accuracy when the information is available on each of the components. Examples of detailed drivers include:

  – **Price per product x volume sold**
  – **# of employees x sales per employee, and**
  – **Average selling price per ton x ton of product of sold**

– **Simple drivers**: When information is scarce or unavailable, choosing one simple driver can be more effective than making assumptions for each component of a detailed driver. An example of a simple driver is an assumed annual sales growth rate.

  – Sales is calculated as:

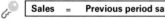

| Sales | = | Previous period sales | x | (1 + Sales growth rate) |

Next, let's flatline a simple driver sales growth rate.

REFER TO SCREENSHOT ON THE RIGHT ⟶

 Please view the Online Companion for related supplementary media.

	Fiscal Year Ending December 31,			Fiscal Year Ending December 31,					5 Year CAGR
	Hist 1	Hist 2	Hist 3	Proj 1	Proj 2	Proj 3	Proj 4	Proj 5	
Sales	$4,172.6	$4,429.2	$4,836.0	$4,981.1	$5,130.5	$5,284.4	$5,442.9	$5,606.2	
Cost of goods sold, excluding depreciation (1)	2,383.7	2,509.2	2,764.7						
Gross profit	1,788.9	1,920.0	2,071.2						
SG&A expenses, excluding amortization	819.5	848.7	895.1						
Other operating (income) / expenses	0.0	0.0	0.0						
EBITDA	969.4	1,071.4	1,176.1						
Depreciation (1)	158.9	171.2	178.3						
Amortization	21.6	18.4	17.9						
EBIT (2)	788.8	881.7	979.9						
Interest expense	65.3	67.9	89.5						
Interest (income)	(1.7)	(1.4)	(1.5)						
Other non-operating (income) / expense	0.0	0.0	0.0						
Pretax income	725.3	815.2	891.9						
Income taxes (3)	266.2	298.4	324.7						
Net income (4)	**$459.1**	**$516.8**	**$567.3**						
Diluted weighted average shares in millions	264.532	256.934	248.292						
Earnings per share	**$1.74**	**$2.01**	**$2.28**						
Ratios & assumptions									
Sales growth rate		6.2%	9.2%	3.0%	3.0%	3.0%	3.0%	3.0%	
Gross margin	42.9%	43.3%	42.8%						
SG&A expenses (as a % of sales)	19.6%	19.2%	18.5%						
Other operating (income) / expenses ($ amount)	$0.0	$0.0	$0.0						
Other non-operating (income) / expense ($ amount)	0.0	0.0	0.0						
Effective tax rate	36.7%	36.6%	36.4%						

Forecasts

Drivers based on inputted assumptions

Only one BLUE input cell if a constant growth rate

Flatline BLACK references: set equal to previous year if kept constant

NOTES

STEP 6

Project operating expenses
down to EBITDA

NOTES

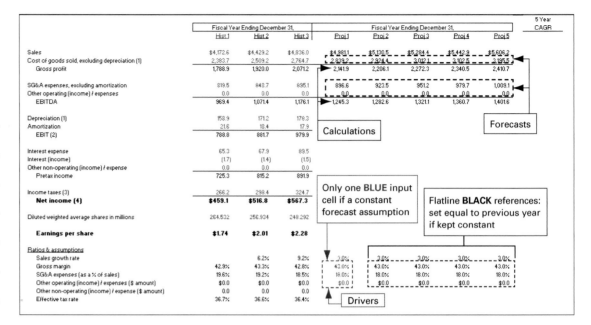

	Fiscal Year Ending December 31,			Fiscal Year Ending December 31,					5 Year CAGR
	Hist 1	Hist 2	Hist 3	Proj 1	Proj 2	Proj 3	Proj 4	Proj 5	
Sales	$4,172.6	$4,429.2	$4,836.0	$4,981.1	$5,130.5	$5,284.4	$5,442.9	$5,606.2	
Cost of goods sold, excluding depreciation (1)	2,383.7	2,509.2	2,764.7	2,839.2	2,924.4	3,012.1	3,102.5	3,195.5	
Gross profit	1,788.9	1,920.0	2,071.2	2,141.9	2,206.1	2,272.3	2,340.5	2,410.7	
SG&A expenses, excluding amortization	819.5	848.7	895.1	896.6	923.5	951.2	979.7	1,009.1	
Other operating (income) / expenses	0.0	0.0	0.0	0.0	0.0	0.0	0.0	0.0	
EBITDA	969.4	1,071.4	1,176.1	1,245.3	1,282.6	1,321.1	1,360.7	1,401.6	
Depreciation (1)	158.9	171.2	178.3						
Amortization	21.6	18.4	17.9						
EBIT (2)	788.8	881.7	979.9						
Interest expense	65.3	67.9	89.5						
Interest (income)	(1.7)	(1.4)	(1.5)						
Other non-operating (income) / expense	0.0	0.0	0.0						
Pretax income	725.3	815.2	891.9						
Income taxes (3)	266.2	298.4	324.7						
Net income (4)	**$459.1**	**$516.8**	**$567.3**						
Diluted weighted average shares in millions	264.532	256.934	248.292						
Earnings per share	**$1.74**	**$2.01**	**$2.28**						
Ratios & assumptions									
Sales growth rate		6.2%	9.2%	3.0%	3.0%	3.0%	3.0%	3.0%	
Gross margin	42.9%	43.3%	42.8%	43.0%	43.0%	43.0%	43.0%	43.0%	
SG&A expenses (as a % of sales)	19.6%	19.2%	18.5%	18.0%	18.0%	18.0%	18.0%	18.0%	
Other operating (income) / expenses ($ amount)	$0.0	$0.0	$0.0	$0.0	$0.0	$0.0	$0.0	$0.0	
Other non-operating (income) / expense ($ amount)	0.0	0.0	0.0						
Effective tax rate	36.7%	36.6%	36.4%						

Forecasts

Calculations

Only one BLUE input cell if a constant forecast assumption

Flatline BLACK references: set equal to previous year if kept constant

Drivers

Forecast operating expenses (cost of goods sold, SG&A) by **flatlining** margin assumptions, for example, gross margin or SG&A as a percentage of sales.

– Cost of goods sold is calculated as:

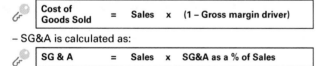

Cost of Goods Sold	=	Sales	x	(1 – Gross margin driver)

– SG&A is calculated as:

SG & A	=	Sales	x	SG&A as a % of Sales

Use historical data or research reports to obtain guidance on appropriate assumptions for drivers.

– Remember, the key question to ask is: Are the chosen assumptions reasonable and defensible?

The line item *other operating expenses/(income)* is usually forecast as a number, based on research or historical data, because it is a mixture of income and expense items that, together, are difficult to project as a percentage of sales (or of any other item).

Calculate down to EBITDA, but leave depreciation and amortization blank for now. Depreciation and amortization expenses will be referenced from separate, supporting schedules once they are completed.

Please view the Online Companion for related supplementary media.

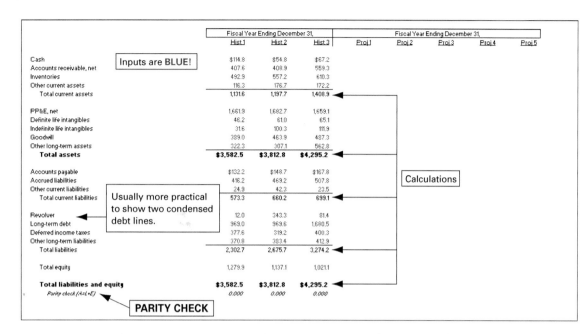

| | Fiscal Year Ending December 31, | | | Fiscal Year Ending December 31, | | | | |
	Hist 1	Hist 2	Hist 3	Proj 1	Proj 2	Proj 3	Proj 4	Proj 5
Cash [Inputs are BLUE!]	$114.8	$54.8	$67.2					
Accounts receivable, net	407.6	408.9	559.3					
Inventories	492.9	557.2	610.3					
Other current assets	116.3	176.7	172.2					
Total current assets	1,131.6	1,197.7	1,408.9					
PP&E, net	1,661.9	1,682.7	1,659.1					
Definite life intangibles	46.2	61.0	65.1					
Indefinite life intangibles	31.6	100.3	111.9					
Goodwill	389.0	463.9	487.3					
Other long-term assets	322.3	307.1	562.8					
Total assets	**$3,582.5**	**$3,812.8**	**$4,295.2**					
Accounts payable	$132.2	$148.7	$167.8					
Accrued liabilities	416.2	469.2	507.8					
Other current liabilities	24.9	42.3	23.5					
Total current liabilities	573.3	660.2	699.1					
Revolver	12.0	343.3	81.4					
Long-term debt	969.0	969.6	1,680.5					
Deferred income taxes	377.6	319.2	400.3					
Other long-term liabilities	370.8	383.4	412.9					
Total liabilities	2,302.7	2,675.7	3,274.2					
Total equity	1,279.9	1,137.1	1,021.1					
Total liabilities and equity	**$3,582.5**	**$3,812.8**	**$4,295.2**					
Parity check (A=L+E)	*0.000*	*0.000*	*0.000*					

[Calculations]

[Usually more practical to show two condensed debt lines.]

PARITY CHECK

NOTES ....

Use company filings or company-provided financial reports to input the historical balance sheet data.

– Form 10-K filings and annual reports provide historical annual data.

Remember, we recommend separating intangible items into three categories: goodwill, definite life intangibles, and indefinite life intangibles. We'll discuss this concept further when we get to the amortization and other long-term items schedules.

Also keep in mind that, in our suggested layout, there is no debt under current liabilities (see Step 2).

Make sure the historical numbers balance:

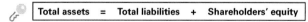

Total assets = Total liabilities + Shareholders' equity

– If you simplify or consolidate line items, be careful not to omit anything. Regardless of how you present them, the value of all items must be captured to ensure parity.

Do not proceed until your three historical years balance and you see 0.000 in the **PARITY CHECK** line.

A = L + E

🖱 **Please view the Online Companion for related supplementary media.**

Flow-of-funds

Stress Testing

Now that we have finished setting up the core statements, let's do some stress testing to make sure the model is functioning correctly.

Income statement

- Go to your *sales driver* cell. Increase the sales growth rate. Did the flatlines work? Did sales increase?

- Now, try inputting a negative sales growth rate. Next, try a zero sales growth rate. Are the results what you expected?

- Go to your *gross margin driver* cell. Change the driver to 100%. Does gross profit = sales? Change the driver to 0%. Does COGS = sales?

- Go to your *projected SG&A expense* cell. Is this value projected correctly (i.e., derived using a margin) or incorrectly (i.e., based on a growth rate)?

Balance sheet

- Does your calculation of total assets include current assets?

- Does your calculation of total liabilities include current liabilities?

- Are you in parity (i.e., do Assets = Liabilities + Equity)? Verify that the "check" line item at the bottom of your balance sheet = 0.000.

If your model passes these basic stress tests, you are in good shape. It doesn't necessarily mean your model is free of errors, but you are headed in the right direction. Its major components are working properly.

 Please view the Online Companion for related supplementary media.

4.2 WORKING CAPITAL SCHEDULE

Typically, there are several funding sources which companies use to fuel organic growth:

- Short-term growth: Working capital.

- Long-term growth: Purchases of property, plant, and equipment or intangibles.

The working capital schedule is used to examine how a company funds its short-term growth. **Working capital** is defined as total current assets (for example, inventory) less total current liabilities (for example, accounts payable).

Working capital	=	Total current assets	−	Total current liabilities

For reasons we're about to explain, we want to examine a particular type of working capital called **net working capital** or **net working investment**. This is defined as total non-cash current assets less total non-debt current liabilities.

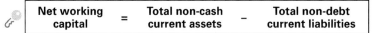

Net working capital	=	Total non-cash current assets	–	Total non-debt current liabilities

We focus on net working capital (instead of regular working capital) for two main reasons:

- This allows us to isolate our analysis of <u>operating working capital</u> without considering the effects of cash or financing.

- From a practical standpoint, we don't want to forecast cash or debt on this schedule because these items are better forecasted on separate schedules. Later, we will forecast cash on the cash flow statement, and use a dedicated debt and interest schedule to project debt.

Be careful! Financial statement/ratios analyses typically employ the traditional working capital definition. Consider showing both versions of working capital using a separate ratios page. But above all, be consistent in your analysis.

Please view the Online Companion for related supplementary media.

STEP 8

Set up the working capital schedule

NOTES

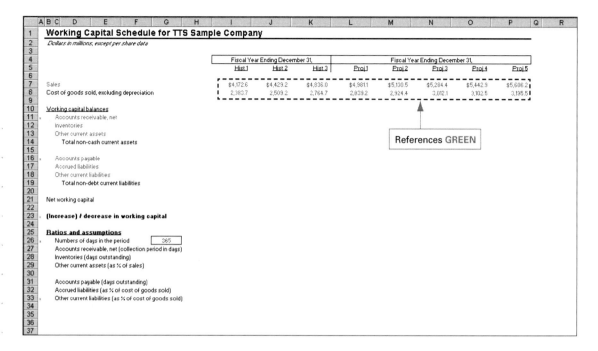

The schedule shows "Working Capital Schedule for TTS Sample Company" with the following row items:

	Fiscal Year Ending December 31,			Fiscal Year Ending December 31,				
	Hist 1	Hist 2	Hist 3	Proj 1	Proj 2	Proj 3	Proj 4	Proj 5
Sales	$4,172.6	$4,429.2	$4,836.0	$4,981.1	$5,130.5	$5,284.4	$5,442.9	$5,606.2
Cost of goods sold, excluding depreciation	2,380.7	2,509.2	2,764.7	2,839.2	2,924.4	3,012.1	3,102.5	3,195.5

References GREEN

Working capital balances
- Accounts receivable, net
- Inventories
- Other current assets
- Total non-cash current assets

- Accounts payable
- Accrued liabilities
- Other current liabilities
- Total non-debt current liabilities

Net working capital

(Increase) / decrease in working capital

Ratios and assumptions
- Numbers of days in the period — 365
- Accounts receivable, net (collection period in days)
- Inventories (days outstanding)
- Other current assets (as % of sales)

- Accounts payable (days outstanding)
- Accrued liabilities (as % of cost of goods sold)
- Other current liabilities (as % of cost of goods sold)

Usually schedules begin with a **relationship driver**. This is a line item that is related to the items about to be forecast. For example, sales is closely related to accounts receivable. As you sell a product on credit, your accounts receivable balance increases. A similar relationship can be drawn between COGS and inventory. As you sell a product, you remove it from your inventory and expense it, which generates cost of goods sold.

– Reference the sales and COGS line items from the income statement on this schedule, as they will be used in calculating ratios and projecting future balances.

– Keep in mind that references from another schedule/sheet should be color-coded green.

Use the same line items as shown on the balance sheet.

– To be efficient, keep line items in the same order as they appear on the balance sheet.

– Separate working capital assets from working capital liabilities. Keep in mind that we're typically concerned with non-cash current assets and non-debt current liabilities on this schedule. We will tackle cash and debt in subsequent schedules.

 Please view the Online Companion for related supplementary media.

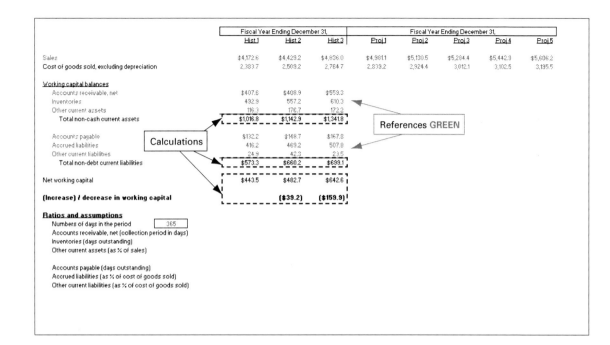

NOTES

Historical balances on this schedule should be linked in from the balance sheet (green references). Do **not** input the balances again on this sheet.

 – Linking to the balance sheet not only saves time but also makes the model more accurate and dynamic, allowing for greater flexibility.

Calculate historical net working capital.

 – Net working capital is calculated as:

| Net working capital | = | Total non-cash current assets | – | Total non-debt current liabilities |

Calculate the increase/decrease in working capital

 – It may help you conceptually to think of this line item as the "cash flow impact from change in working capital."

 – In this calculation, increases in net working capital are shown as <u>negative</u>. That's because, from a cash flow perspective, an increase in net working capital assets represents a <u>use of cash</u>.

STEP 10

Calculate the historical ratios for each working capital line item

In this step, we will correlate the working capital line items with two relationship drivers: sales, and cost of goods sold.

- There are various ways to examine the correlation between accounts receivable, inventory, and accounts payable, and their relationship drivers. One way is to look at **turnover calculations**, such as **inventory turns**, which measures how many times the company sells through all of its inventory in a given period. It is calculated as:

$$\text{Inventory turns} = \frac{\text{Cost of sales}}{\text{Inventory balance}}$$

We will calculate various **days formulas**, which is a typical way of analyzing working capital. For this, you can use either ending balances or average balances. Either is acceptable as long as you are consistent. For training purposes, we will use ending balances.

- **Accounts receivable days** is calculated by dividing the accounts receivable balance for a given period by the sales over that same period, then multiplying that quantity by the number of days being modeled. (For an annual model, this number is typically 365 or 360.)

$$\text{Accounts receivable days} = \frac{\text{Accounts receivable balance for a given period}}{\text{Sales over that same period}} \times \text{Number of days being modeled}$$

Accounts receivable days measures how many days it takes a company to collect cash from its customers

- **Inventories days outstanding** is calculated by dividing the inventories balance for a given period by the COGS over that same period and multiplying that quantity by the number of days being modeled.

$$\text{Inventories days outstanding} = \frac{\text{Inventories balance for a given period}}{\text{COGS over that same period}} \times \text{Number of days being modeled}$$

Inventories days outstanding measures the number of days it takes the company to turnover its inventory.

- **Accounts payable days** is calculated similarly to accounts receivable, except that the accounts payable balance is divided by COGS before it is multiplied by the number of days being modeled.

$$\text{Accounts payable days} = \frac{\text{Accounts payable balance for a given period}}{\text{COGS over that same period}} \times \text{Number of days being modeled}$$

Accounts payable days measures how many days it takes a company to pay cash to its suppliers.

For simplicity, other working capital ratios are typically calculated as percentages of either sales or cost of sales.

- For example, other current assets as a percentage of sales is calculated by dividing the other current assets balance for a given period by the sales over that same period.

Please view the Online Companion for related supplementary media.

REFER TO SCREENSHOT ON THE RIGHT ⟶

	Fiscal Year Ending December 31,			Fiscal Year Ending December 31,				
	Hist 1	Hist 2	Hist 3	Proj 1	Proj 2	Proj 3	Proj 4	Proj 5
Sales	$4,172.6	$4,429.2	$4,836.0	$4,981.1	$5,130.5	$5,284.4	$5,442.9	$5,606.2
Cost of goods sold, excluding depreciation	2,383.7	2,509.2	2,764.7	2,839.2	2,924.4	3,012.1	3,102.5	3,195.5
Working capital balances								
Accounts receivable, net	$407.6	$408.9	$559.3					
Inventories	492.9	557.2	610.3					
Other current assets	116.3	176.7	172.2					
Total non-cash current assets	$1,016.8	$1,142.9	$1,341.8					
Accounts payable	$132.2	$148.7	$167.8					
Accrued liabilities	416.2	469.2	507.8					
Other current liabilities	24.9	42.3	23.5					
Total non-debt current liabilities	$573.3	$660.2	$699.1					
Net working capital	$443.5	$482.7	$642.6					
(Increase) / decrease in working capital		($39.2)	($159.9)					

Ratios and assumptions

Numbers of days in the period	365	← cell is named "Days"						
Accounts receivable, net (collection period in days)	35.7	33.7	42.2					
Inventories (days outstanding)	75.5	81.0	80.6					
Other current assets (as % of sales)	2.8%	4.0%	3.6%					
Accounts payable (days outstanding)	20.2	21.6	22.2					
Accrued liabilities (as % of cost of goods sold)	17.5%	18.7%	18.4%					
Other current liabilities (as % of cost of goods sold)	1.0%	1.7%	0.8%					

Calculations

NOTES ·················

	Fiscal Year Ending December 31,			Fiscal Year Ending December 31,				
	Hist 1	Hist 2	Hist 3	Proj 1	Proj 2	Proj 3	Proj 4	Proj 5
Sales	$4,172.6	$4,429.2	$4,836.0	$4,981.1	$5,130.5	$5,284.4	$5,442.9	$5,606.2
Cost of goods sold, excluding depreciation	2,383.7	2,509.2	2,764.7	2,839.2	2,924.4	3,012.1	3,102.5	3,195.5
Working capital balances								
Accounts receivable, net	$407.6	$408.9	$559.3					
Inventories	492.9	557.2	610.3					
Other current assets	116.3	176.7	172.2					
Total non-cash current assets	$1,016.8	$1,142.9	$1,341.8					
Accounts payable	$132.2	$148.7	$167.8					
Accrued liabilities	416.2	469.2	507.3					
Other current liabilities	24.9	42.3	23.5					
Total non-debt current liabilities	$573.3	$660.2	$699.1					
Net working capital	$443.5	$482.7	$642.6					
(Increase) / decrease in working capital		($39.2)	($159.9)					
Ratios and assumptions								
Numbers of days in the period		365						
Accounts receivable, net (collection period in days)	35.7	33.7	42.2	42.0	42.0	42.0	42.0	42.0
Inventories (days outstanding)	75.5	81.0	80.6	80.5	80.5	80.5	80.5	80.5
Other current assets (as % of sales)	2.8%	4.0%	3.6%	3.6%	3.6%	3.6%	3.6%	3.6%
Accounts payable (days outstanding)	20.2	21.6	22.2	22.0	22.0	22.0	22.0	22.0
Accrued liabilities (as % of cost of goods sold)	17.5%	18.7%	18.4%	18.4%	18.4%	18.4%	18.4%	18.4%
Other current liabilities (as % of cost of goods sold)	1.0%	1.7%	0.8%	0.8%	0.8%	0.8%	0.8%	0.8%

Flatline **BLACK** references:
set equal to previous year
if kept constant

Assumptions: make only
first number **BLUE** input

Make reasonable assumptions to project each working capital balance.

– Use historical data, management guidance, and research reports to guide your assumptions.

··

Some items that do not have an obvious driver or relationship to sales or COGS may be held constant in projected years
(for example, other current assets).

··

The assumption used in the first projected year will act as your driver and should therefore be color-coded blue. For simplicity, we will assume
that subsequent projected years have the same assumptions as the first projected year. To model this assumption, simply flatline the formula
back to the previous year.

 Please view the Online Companion for related supplementary media.

NOTES

STEP 12

Use the assumptions made in Step 11 to forecast each of the working capital balances.

— Some items will be forecasted as a percentage of sales or COGS.

— For accounts receivable, inventory, and accounts payable, you will need to imply projected dollar amounts.

— Recall the formula for accounts receivable days:

$$\text{Accounts Receivable days} = \frac{\text{Accounts Receivable \$}}{\text{Sales}} \times \text{Number of days}$$

— This relationship still holds, but in this case we are solving for the forecasted dollar amount of accounts receivable. If you rewrite the equation, the forecasted dollar amount of accounts receivable becomes:

$$\text{\$ Accounts Receivable} = \frac{(\text{Accounts Receivable days driver} \times \text{Sales})}{\text{Number of days}}$$

— Forecasted dollar amount of inventory is:

$$\text{\$ Inventory} = \frac{(\text{Inventory days driver} \times \text{COGS})}{\text{Number of days}}$$

— Forecasted dollar amount of accounts payable is:

$$\text{\$ Accounts Payable} = \frac{(\text{Accounts Payable days driver} \times \text{COGS})}{\text{Number of days}}$$

Once you've finished projecting these balances, take a step back and ask yourself: Do these numbers seem reasonable?

— As a guide, compare your forecasted dollar amounts to balances and trends across the historical years.

REFER TO SCREENSHOT ON THE RIGHT $\longrightarrow$

Please view the Online Companion for related supplementary media.

	Fiscal Year Ending December 31,			Fiscal Year Ending December 31,				
	Hist 1	Hist 2	Hist 3	Proj 1	Proj 2	Proj 3	Proj 4	Proj 5
Sales	$4,172.6	$4,429.2	$4,836.0	$4,981.1	$5,130.5	$5,284.4	$5,442.9	$5,606.2
Cost of goods sold, excluding depreciation	2,383.7	2,509.2	2,764.7	2,839.2	2,924.4	3,012.1	3,102.5	3,195.5
Working capital balances								
Accounts receivable, net	$407.6	$408.9	$559.3	$573.2	$590.4	$608.1	$626.3	$645.1
Inventories	492.9	557.2	610.3	626.2	645.0	664.3	684.2	704.8
Other current assets	116.3	176.7	172.2	179.3	184.7	190.2	195.9	201.8
Total non-cash current assets	$1,016.8	$1,142.9	$1,341.8					
Accounts payable	$132.2	$148.7	$167.8	$171.1	$176.3	$181.6	$187.0	$192.6
Accrued liabilities	416.2	469.2	507.8	522.4	538.1	554.2	570.9	588.0
Other current liabilities	24.9	42.3	23.5	22.7	23.4	24.1	24.8	25.6
Total non-debt current liabilities	$573.3	$660.2	$699.1					
Net working capital	$443.5	$482.7	$642.6					
(Increase) / decrease in working capital		**($39.2)**	**($159.9)**					
Ratios and assumptions								
Numbers of days in the period `365`								
Accounts receivable, net (collection period in days)	35.7	33.7	42.2	42.0	42.0	42.0	42.0	42.0
Inventories (days outstanding)	75.5	81.0	80.6	80.5	80.5	80.5	80.5	80.5
Other current assets (as % of sales)	2.8%	4.0%	3.6%	3.6%	3.6%	3.6%	3.6%	3.6%
Accounts payable (days outstanding)	20.2	21.6	22.2	22.0	22.0	22.0	22.0	22.0
Accrued liabilities (as % of cost of goods sold)	17.5%	18.7%	18.4%	18.4%	18.4%	18.4%	18.4%	18.4%
Other current liabilities (as % of cost of goods sold)	1.0%	1.7%	0.8%	0.8%	0.8%	0.8%	0.8%	0.8%

Drivers

Projections

Drivers

NOTES

....

....

....

....

STEP 13

Finish the working capital schedule

NOTES

	Fiscal Year Ending December 31,			Fiscal Year Ending December 31,				
	Hist 1	Hist 2	Hist 3	Proj 1	Proj 2	Proj 3	Proj 4	Proj 5
Sales	$4,172.6	$4,429.2	$4,836.0	$4,981.1	$5,130.5	$5,284.4	$5,442.9	$5,606.2
Cost of goods sold, excluding depreciation	2,383.7	2,509.2	2,764.7	2,839.2	2,924.4	3,012.1	3,102.5	3,195.5
Working capital balances								
Accounts receivable, net	$407.6	$408.9	$559.3	$573.2	$590.4	$608.1	$626.3	$645.1
Inventories	492.9	557.2	610.3	626.2	645.0	664.3	684.2	704.8
Other current assets	116.3	176.7	172.2	179.3	184.7	190.2	195.9	201.8
Total non-cash current	$1,016.8	$1,142.9	$1,341.8	$1,378.7	$1,420.0	$1,462.6	$1,506.5	$1,551.7
Accounts payable	$132.2	$148.7	$167.9	$171.1	$176.3	$181.6	$187.0	$192.6
Accrued liabilities	416.2	469.2	507.3	522.4	538.1	554.2	570.9	588.0
Other current liabilities	24.9	42.3	23.5	22.7	23.4	24.1	24.8	25.6
Total non-debt current liabilities	$573.3	$660.2	$699.1	$716.3	$737.7	$759.9	$782.7	$806.2
Net working capital	$443.5	$482.7	$642.6	$662.4	$682.3	$702.7	$723.8	$745.5
(Increase) / decrease in working capital		($39.2)	($159.9)	($19.8)	($19.9)	($20.5)	($21.1)	($21.7)
Ratios and assumptions								
Numbers of days in the period [365]								
Accounts receivable, net (collection period in days)	35.7	33.7	42.2	42.0	42.0	42.0	42.0	42.0
Inventories (days outstanding)	75.5	81.0	80.6	80.5	80.5	80.5	80.5	80.5
Other current assets (as % of sales)	2.8%	4.0%	3.6%	3.6%	3.6%	3.6%	3.6%	3.6%
Accounts payable (days outstanding)	20.2	21.6	22.2	22.0	22.0	22.0	22.0	22.0
Accrued liabilities (as % of cost of goods sold)	17.5%	18.7%	18.4%	18.4%	18.4%	18.4%	18.4%	18.4%
Other current liabilities (as % of cost of goods sold)	1.0%	1.7%	0.8%	0.8%	0.8%	0.8%	0.8%	0.8%

Right border on the last historical year as a "divider". Make this the **LAST** thing you do on the schedule!

Calculations

Calculate totals for non-cash current assets and total non-debt current liabilities.

Calculate net working capital and the (Increase)/decrease in working capital.

Check again for consistency between historical and projected trends.

– Large increases or decreases may represent an error in calculation. If your calculations are working properly, consider tweaking your assumptions to help 'smooth' the trend.

Add a right border to separate the historical and projected periods.

	Fiscal Year Ending December 31,			Fiscal Year Ending December 31,				
	Hist 1	Hist 2	Hist 3	Proj 1	Proj 2	Proj 3	Proj 4	Proj 5
Cash	$114.8	$54.8	$67.2					
Accounts receivable, net	407.6	408.9	559.3	573.2	590.4	608.1	626.3	645.1
Inventories	492.9	557.2	610.3	626.2	645.0	664.3	684.2	704.8
Other current assets	116.3	176.7	172.2	179.3	184.7	190.2	195.9	201.8
Total current assets	1,131.6	1,197.7	1,408.9					
PP&E, net	1,661.9	1,682.7	1,653.1					
Definite life intangibles	46.2	61.0	65.1					
Indefinite life intangibles	31.6	100.3	111.9					
Goodwill	389.0	463.9	487.3					
Other long-term assets	322.3	307.1	562.8					
Total assets	**$3,582.5**	**$3,812.8**	**$4,295.2**					
Accounts payable	$132.2	$148.7	$167.8	$171.1	$176.3	$181.6	$187.0	$192.6
Accrued liabilities	416.2	469.2	507.8	522.4	538.1	554.2	570.9	588.0
Other current liabilities	24.9	42.3	23.5	22.7	23.4	24.1	24.8	25.6
Total current liabilities	573.3	660.2	699.1					
Revolver	12.0	343.3	81.4					
Long-term debt	969.0	969.6	1,680.5					
Deferred income taxes	377.6	319.2	400.3					
Other long-term liabilities	370.8	383.4	412.9					
Total liabilities	2,302.7	2,675.7	3,274.2					
Total equity	1,279.9	1,137.1	1,021.1					
Total liabilities and equity	**$3,582.5**	**$3,812.8**	**$4,295.2**					
Parity check (A=L+E)	0.000	0.000	0.000					

References GREEN

NOTES

Now that the working capital schedule is complete, link the *projected years for each of the working capital accounts* to the balance sheet.

– Remember, we created line items on the working capital schedule in the same order as they appear on the balance sheet to speed up this process. Be efficient!

NOTES ....

....

....

....

....

....

....

	Fiscal Year Ending December 31,				
	Proj 1	Proj 2	Proj 3	Proj 4	Proj 5
Operating activities					
Net income					
Stock-based compensation expense					
Depreciation	Historicals not needed				
Amortization					
(Increase) / decrease in working capital		(19.8)	(19.3)	(20.5)	(21.1)	(21.7)
Change in other long-term assets and liabilities					
Cash flow from operating activities					
Investing activities					
Capital expenditures					
Additions to definite life intangibles					
Cash flow from investing activities	References GREEN				
Cash flow available for financing activities					
Financing activities					
Issuance / (repayment) of revolver					
Issuance of long-term debt					
(Repayment) of long-term debt					
Repurchase of equity					
Dividends					
Option proceeds					
Cash flow from financing activities					
Net change in cash					
Beginning cash balance					
Ending cash balance					

Link the (Increase)/decrease in working capital line on the cash flow statement to the (Increase)/decrease in working capital line on the working capital schedule.

....

Remember, an increase in net working capital should be shown as a <u>negative</u> number to signify a use of cash; a decrease in net working capital should be shown as a <u>positive</u> number to signify a source of cash.

Flow-of-funds

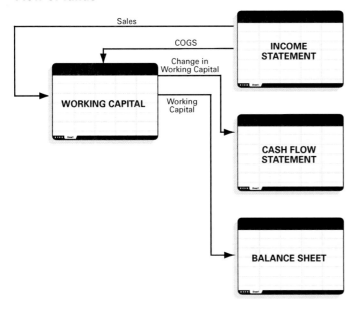

Stress Testing

Now that we've finished setting up the working capital schedule, let's do some stress testing to ensure everything is working properly.

We will focus our stress test on accounts receivable, which is a common working capital item across companies.

To test the accounts receivable driver:

- Go to your *accounts receivable days driver cell*, and change it to zero. Did your flatlines work (i.e., did accounts receivable days change to zero in projected years)?

- Check the dollar amounts of projected accounts receivable balances. Did they zero out, too?

- Keeping all other drivers and cells constant, if you were to increase the accounts receivable driver, what would be the impact to cash flow be?

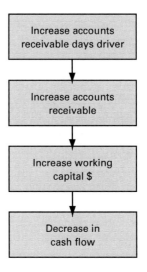

 Please view the Online Companion for related supplementary media.

4.3 DEPRECIATION SCHEDULE

One way for a company to fund its long-term growth is to purchase property, plant, and equipment (PP&E). Recall our previous identification of funding sources:

- Short-term growth: Working capital

- Long-term growth: Purchases of PP&E and intangibles

Purchases (of PP&E) are generally referred to as capital expenditures (CapEx). A basic assumption on this schedule is that a company needs to maintain a certain level of CapEx to support its long-term sales growth. So to get started on this schedule, the first thing we'll do after setting up our line items is reference the company's *sales* from the income statement. We will use *sales* to drive our projection of CapEx.

To find the company's historical CapEx numbers, you'll need to reference the company's annual filing, so have that ready to go. (The annual filing is included in the Case Study, and it's downloadable online.) After we enter historical information, we will project capital expenditures, depreciation expense, and property, plant, and equipment balances.

Depreciation Schedule for TTS Sample Company

Dollars in millions, except per share data

		Fiscal Year Ending December 31,			Fiscal Year Ending December 31,				
		Hist 1	Hist 2	Hist 3	Proj 1	Proj 2	Proj 3	Proj 4	Proj 5
Sales		$4,172.6	$4,429.2	$4,836.0	$4,981.1	$5,100.5	$5,284.4	$5,442.9	$5,606.2
Capital expenditures		218.7	181.7	181.1					
Capital expenditures as % of sales		*5.2%*	*4.1%*	*3.7%*					
Depreciation expense									
Depreciation as % of capex									
Depreciation as % of PP&E, net									
Beginning PP&E, net									
Capital expenditures									
(Depreciation expense)									
(Asset sales and write-offs)									
Ending PP&E, net									

Input historical CapEx (BLUE)

Calculations

References GREEN

Set up the line items as shown above.

Reference sales from the income statement, including both historical and projected values.

– We use sales to drive our projection of capital expenditures (CapEx) because we assume the company will need to purchase property, plant, and equipment (PP&E) to support long-term sales growth.

Input historical CapEx numbers on a line just below sales.

– These numbers can typically be found on the company's cash flow statement. CapEx can be found under the investing activities section (usually located in the middle of the cash flow statement).

Calculate historical CapEx as a percentage of sales.

– This can be an important item to examine: As the company grows more quickly and its sales increase, it will likely need to spend more money on capital such as machines and other equipment to support its growing business.

	Fiscal Year Ending December 31,			Fiscal Year Ending December 31,				
	Hist 1	Hist 2	Hist 3	Proj 1	Proj 2	Proj 3	Proj 4	Proj 5
Sales	$4,172.6	$4,429.2	$4,836.0	$4,981.1	$5,130.5	$5,284.4	$5,442.9	$5,606.2
Capital expenditures	218.7	181.7	181.1	195.0	189.8	195.5	201.4	207.4
Capital expenditures as % of sales	5.2%	4.1%	3.7%	3.9%	3.7%	3.7%	3.7%	3.7%
Depreciation expense								
Depreciation as % of capex								
Depreciation as % of PP&E, net								
Beginning PP&E, net								
Capital expenditures								
(Depreciation expense)								
(Asset sales and write-offs)								
Ending PP&E, net								

Input, usually from research or management

Common driver if projected CapEx is not available

Forecasts

Calculations

To help you project this balance, use a research report, management guidance, or disclosure in an annual filing, such as the Management Discussion & Analysis section (MD&A).

– Sometimes management communicates its expected future capital spending in the MD&A section.

CapEx can be projected in two ways: (1) as a dollar amount or (2) as a percentage of sales.

– **Dollar amount**: This is usually the better way if the company has historically spent the same amount every year, or if management provides specific numbers on how much they expect to spend.

– **As a percentage of sales**: This is the better method if capital expenditures have trended higher with increases in sales, or if management or research offer no guidance..

– Choose a percentage of sales that is reasonable based on historical data.

Typically, management will provide one or two years of guidance in its annual filing. In this example, we inputted (or hard coded) a CapEx projection based on management's guidance in the first projected year. We then switched to a percentage of sales driver since no guidance for subsequent years was available from management. The takeaway: Customize your drivers based on the information available for the specific company you are modeling.

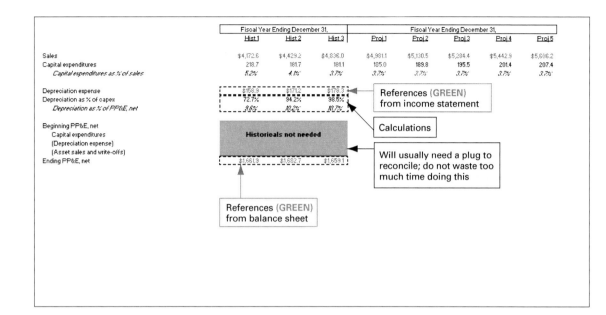

STEP 18
....
Reference historical information
from income statement and
balance sheet

NOTES ....

Link historical depreciation expense from the income statement.

Calculate depreciation as a percentage of CapEx and as a percentage of PP&E, net.

– These can be used as drivers for projecting future depreciation expense.

Link historical PP&E, net from the balance sheet.

– Focus on ending PP&E balances here. Don't worry about modeling the historical items that are used to reconcile this balance (for example, historical asset sales and write-offs). It is typically difficult to reconcile historical PP&E balances because of a lack of information in the financial statements.

NOTES ....

....

....

....

....

	Fiscal Year Ending December 31,			Fiscal Year Ending December 31,				
	Hist 1	Hist 2	Hist 3	Proj 1	Proj 2	Proj 3	Proj 4	Proj 5
Sales	$4,172.6	$4,429.2	$4,836.0	$4,981.1	$5,130.5	$5,284.4	$5,442.9	$5,606.2
Capital expenditures	218.7	181.7	181.1	185.0	189.8	195.5	201.4	207.4
Capital expenditures as % of sales	*5.2%*	*4.1%*	*3.7%*	*3.7%*	*3.7%*	*3.7%*	*3.7%*	*3.7%*
Depreciation expense	$158.9	$171.2	$173.3	$180.0	$187.0	$192.6	$198.4	$204.3
Depreciation as % of capex	72.7%	94.2%	98.5%	97.3%	98.5%	98.5%	98.5%	98.5%
Depreciation as % of PP&E, net	*9.6%*	*10.2%*	*10.7%*					
Beginning PP&E, net								
Capital expenditures								
(Depreciation expense)								
(Asset sales and write-offs)								
Ending PP&E, net	$1,661.9	$1,682.7	$1,659.1					

Forecasts

Common driver if projected depreciation
expense is not available. Review historcials,
research or management expectations.

Here are five different ways to project depreciation expense. Choose a reasonable method based on what you know about the company and its industry.

- **As a percentage of CapEx**: This method works well for modeling mature companies whose projected depreciation roughly equals projected CapEx. This is sometimes referred to as 'maintenance CapEx'—capturing the idea that companies with low growth tend to spend just enough on capital assets to maintain them (that is, to replace what is being depreciated).

- **As a percentage of PP&E**: This method is often effective for companies with short-lived assets, where any increase in PP&E is met by a relative decrease in depreciation.

- **As a percentage of sales**: This method also works well for companies with short-lived assets. However, make sure this assumption is reasonable compared to projected CapEx. For example, it's unlikely that a company will depreciate $100 of assets every year if it's spending only $10 a year on CapEx.

- **Constant/varying dollar amount**: Good for matching research projections.

- **A reasonable growth rate**: If no other method seems quite right, then project a reasonable increase in depreciation expense that is consistent with a normal, growing business.

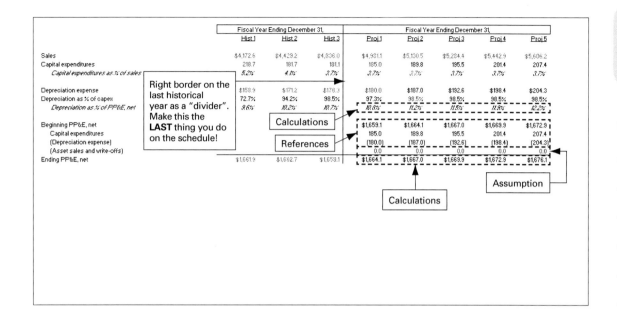

	Fiscal Year Ending December 31,			Fiscal Year Ending December 31,				
	Hist 1	Hist 2	Hist 3	Proj 1	Proj 2	Proj 3	Proj 4	Proj 5
Sales	$4,172.6	$4,423.2	$4,306.0	$4,931.1	$5,130.5	$5,284.4	$5,442.9	$5,606.2
Capital expenditures	218.7	181.7	181.1	185.0	189.8	195.5	201.4	207.4
Capital expenditures as % of sales	*5.2%*	*4.1%*	*3.7%*	*3.7%*	*3.7%*	*3.7%*	*3.7%*	*3.7%*
Depreciation expense	$153.9	$171.2	$178.3	$180.0	$187.0	$192.6	$198.4	$204.3
Depreciation as % of capex	72.7%	94.2%	98.5%	97.3%	98.5%	98.5%	98.5%	98.5%
Depreciation as % of PP&E, net	*9.6%*	*10.2%*	*10.7%*	*10.8%*	*11.2%*	*11.5%*	*11.8%*	*12.2%*
Beginning PP&E, net				$1,659.1	$1,664.1	$1,667.0	$1,669.9	$1,672.9
Capital expenditures				185.0	189.8	195.5	201.4	207.4
(Depreciation expense)				(180.0)	(187.0)	(192.6)	(198.4)	(204.3)
(Asset sales and write-offs)				0.0	0.0	0.0	0.0	0.0
Ending PP&E, net	$1,661.9	$1,692.7	$1,659.1	$1,664.1	$1,667.0	$1,669.9	$1,672.9	$1,676.1

Right border on the last historical year as a "divider". Make this the **LAST** thing you do on the schedule!

Calculations

References

Calculations

Assumption

NOTES ·

The beginning PP&E balance for one period is equal to the ending PP&E balance for the previous year. For example, the PP&E balance on Proj 1 is the same as the PP&E balance on Hist 3.

Reference CapEx from the projections you calculated in Step 17.

    – CapEx is shown as <u>positive</u> here because as a company makes capital investments, its PP&E balance increases.

Reference depreciation expense from the projections you calculated in Step 19.

    – Depreciation is shown as <u>negative</u> here because as a company depreciates assets, its PP&E balance decreases.

Make an assumption regarding future asset sales. If no information is provided by either management or research, then it is common to assume no asset sales.

    – Asset sales, if there are any, are would be shown as <u>negative</u> here because they decrease a company's PP&E balance.

Calculate depreciation as a percentage of PP&E, net for the projected periods.

 Please view the Online Companion for related supplementary media.

STEP 21

Adjust the depreciation projections
to create a "smoothing" effect

NOTES

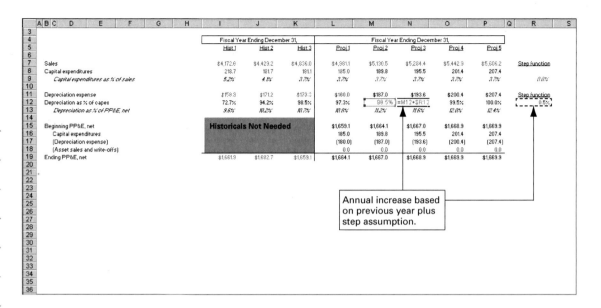

Annual increase based
on previous year plus
step assumption.

Now that the depreciation schedule is complete, determine the appropriate relationship between depreciation and CapEx for the company you are modeling.

- A mature company (that is, one with stable growth) spends just enough on CapEx to maintain or replace its existing PP&E. If the company you are modeling is a mature one, consider making projected depreciation roughly equal to projected CapEx.

- Faster-growing companies (for example, technology firms) spend somewhat more money on new machines and buildings to support their rapid growth. If the company you are modeling is growing quickly, consider making projected depreciation less than projected CapEx.

Incorporating a step function is an effective way to increase or decrease your assumption in projected years.

Use historical relationships between depreciation and CapEx to guide your assumptions.

If available, third-party research projections can also be a useful guide.

 Please view the Online Companion for related supplementary media.

	Fiscal Year Ending December 31,			Fiscal Year Ending December 31,				
	Hist 1	Hist 2	Hist 3	Proj 1	Proj 2	Proj 3	Proj 4	Proj 5
Sales	$4,172.6	$4,429.2	$4,836.0	$4,981.1	$5,130.5	$5,284.4	$5,442.9	$5,606.2
Cost of goods sold, excluding depreciation (1)	2,383.7	2,509.2	2,764.7	2,839.2	2,924.4	3,012.1	3,102.5	3,195.5
Gross profit	1,788.9	1,920.0	2,071.2	2,141.9	2,206.1	2,272.3	2,340.5	2,410.7
SG&A expenses, excluding amortization	819.5	848.7	895.1	896.6	923.5	951.2	979.7	1,009.1
Other operating (income) / expenses	0.0	0.0	0.0	0.0	0.0	0.0	0.0	0.0
EBITDA	969.4	1,071.4	1,176.1	1,245.3	1,282.6	1,321.1	1,360.7	1,401.6
Depreciation (1)	158.9	171.2	178.3	180.0	187.0	193.6	200.4	207.4
Amortization	21.6	18.4	17.9					
EBIT (2)	788.8	881.7	979.9					
Interest expense	65.3	67.9	89.5					
Interest (income)	(1.7)	(1.4)	(1.5)					
Other non-operating (income) / expense	0.0	0.0	0.0					
Pretax income	725.3	815.2	891.9					
Income taxes (3)	266.2	298.4	324.7					
Net income (4)	**$459.1**	**$516.8**	**$567.3**					
Diluted weighted average shares in millions	264.532	256.934	248.292					
Earnings per share	**$1.74**	**$2.01**	**$2.28**					
Ratios & assumptions								
Sales growth rate		6.2%	9.2%	3.0%	3.0%	3.0%	3.0%	3.0%
Gross margin	42.9%	43.3%	42.8%	43.0%	43.0%	43.0%	43.0%	43.0%
SG&A expenses (as a % of sales)	19.6%	19.2%	18.5%	18.0%	18.0%	18.0%	18.0%	18.0%
Other operating (income) / expenses ($ amount)	$0.0	$0.0	$0.0	$0.0	$0.0	$0.0	$0.0	$0.0
Other non-operating (income) / expense ($ amount)	0.0	0.0	0.0					
Effective tax rate	36.7%	36.6%	36.4%					

References

Link projected depreciation expense to the income statement.

– Make sure that you are referencing from the correct years.

STEP 23

Link PP&E projections to the balance sheet

NOTES

	Fiscal Year Ending December 31,			Fiscal Year Ending December 31,				
	Hist 1	Hist 2	Hist 3	Proj 1	Proj 2	Proj 3	Proj 4	Proj 5
Cash	$114.8	$54.8	$67.2					
Accounts receivable, net	407.6	408.9	559.3	573.2	590.4	608.1	626.3	645.1
Inventories	492.9	557.2	610.3	626.2	645.0	664.3	684.2	704.8
Other current assets	116.3	176.7	172.2	179.0	184.7	190.2	195.9	201.8
Total current assets	1,131.6	1,197.7	1,408.9					
PP&E, net	1,661.9	1,682.7	1,859.1	1,664.1	1,667.0	1,668.9	1,669.9	1,669.9
Definite life intangibles	46.2	61.0	65.1					
Indefinite life intangibles	31.6	100.3	111.9					
Goodwill	389.0	463.9	487.3					
Other long-term assets	322.3	307.1	562.8					
Total assets	**$3,582.5**	**$3,812.8**	**$4,295.2**					
Accounts payable	$132.2	$148.7	$167.8	$171.1	$176.3	$181.6	$187.0	$192.6
Accrued liabilities	416.2	469.2	507.8	522.4	538.1	554.2	570.9	588.0
Other current liabilities	24.9	42.3	23.5	22.7	23.4	24.1	24.8	25.6
Total current liabilities	573.3	660.2	699.1					
Revolver	12.0	343.3	81.4					
Long-term debt	969.0	969.6	1,680.5					
Deferred income taxes	377.6	319.2	400.3					
Other long-term liabilities	370.8	383.4	412.9					
Total liabilities	2,302.7	2,675.7	3,274.2					
Total equity	1,279.9	1,137.1	1,021.1					
Total liabilities and equity	**$3,582.5**	**$3,812.8**	**$4,295.2**					
Parity check (A=L+E)	*0.000*	*0.000*	*0.000*					

References

Link the projected ending PP&E, net balance to the balance sheet.

– Remember that the balance sheet represents values at one particular point in time: the last day of the period (for example, Hist 3).

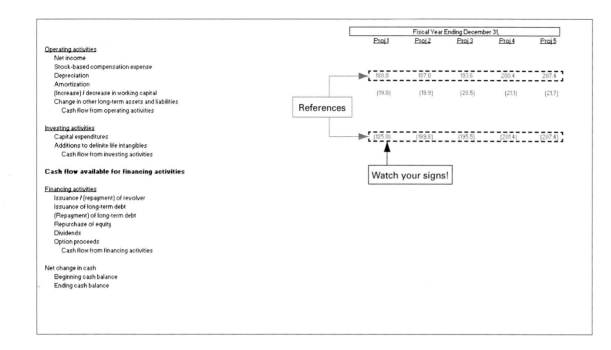

Link projected depreciation expense to the cash flow statement. Be careful to link to the proper row—that is, toward the top of the sheet.

– Remember that depreciation expense should be shown as <u>positive</u> here, because it is being added back to net income as a non-cash expense.

Link projected capital expenditures to the cash flow statement (middle of the page, under investing activities).

– Remember that CapEx should be shown as negative here, because CapEx is a cash outflow.

Flow-of-funds

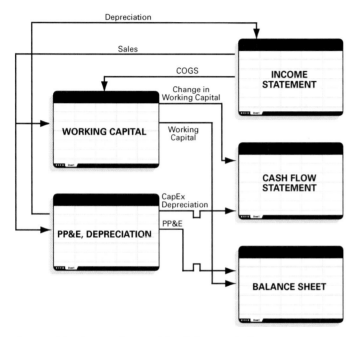

Stress Testing – "Smoothing" Depreciation

Depreciation expense and CapEx are inextricably linked. Depreciation as a percentage of CapEx can be a useful measure of where a company is in its lifecycle. Generally, there are three possible scenarios:

Depreciation as a % of CapEx	Stage in Lifecycle
< 100%	Growth
> 100%	Decline
~ 100%	Mature/steady growth

A company whose depreciation as a percentage of CapEx is <u>less than</u> 100% is adding to its capital base (i.e., increasing its existing PP&E balance) faster than it is depreciating it. Such a company is likely to be in a growth phase and is purchasing assets to fund its growth.

A company whose depreciation as a percentage of CapEx is <u>greater than</u> 100% is depreciating its capital base (i.e., decreasing its existing PP&E balance) faster than it is adding to it. Such a company is likely to be mature, meaning it has moved beyond its growth phase. If the relationship persists, however, it could mean that the company is in a state of decline.

A company whose depreciation as a percentage of CapEx is <u>approximately equal to</u> 100% is purchasing just enough assets to replace those assets that have depreciated. Such a company is likely to be mature and is using CapEx to "maintain" a certain level of growth.

Be sure to evaluate your target company's profile in determining an appropriate level of depreciation as a percentage of CapEx . Where is the company in its lifecycle and where do you expect it to be in a few years? Are you modeling a fast-rising technology company with a dynamic growth story that just went public? Or are you modeling a century-old industrial stalwart with steady cash flows? Use the answers to these questions to help you determine an appropriate driver.

 Please view the Online Companion for related supplementary media.

4.4 AMORTIZATION SCHEDULE

Recall that a company has several sources for funding growth:

- Short term growth: Working capital.

- Long term growth: Purchases of PP&E or intangibles.

The purpose of the amortization schedule is to forecast the value of definite life intangibles. These are assets that have a fixed useful life and are subject to amortization, such as acquired patents. We will handle the other types of intangible assets (for example, indefinite life intangibles and goodwill) on the next supporting schedule.

To get started on this schedule, we first set up the line items. We then reference *sales* from the income statement. As we did on our depreciation schedule, we assume that to maintain a certain rate of sales growth, a company needs to spend a certain amount on additions to definite life intangibles.

 Please view the Online Companion for related supplementary media.

STEP 25

······························

Set up the amortization schedule

NOTES ···························

···

···

···

···

···

···

···

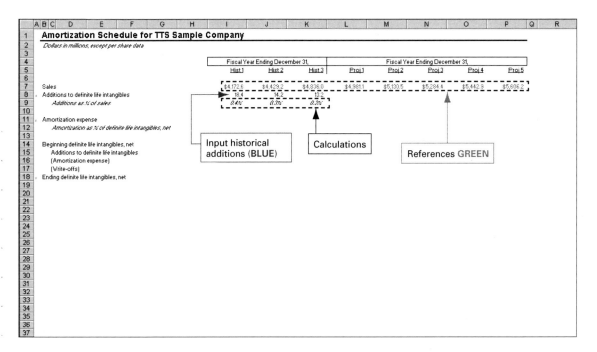

Set up the line items as shown. Most will be similar to the depreciation schedule.

Reference *sales* from the income statement, including both historical and projected values.

Input historical additions to definite life intangibles on a line just below sales.

– These numbers can be found in company filings or company-provided financial reports . You'll find them on the cash flow statement, under the Investing Activities section. (Look in the middle of the cash flow statement.) Alternatively, they may be labeled as purchases of intangibles.

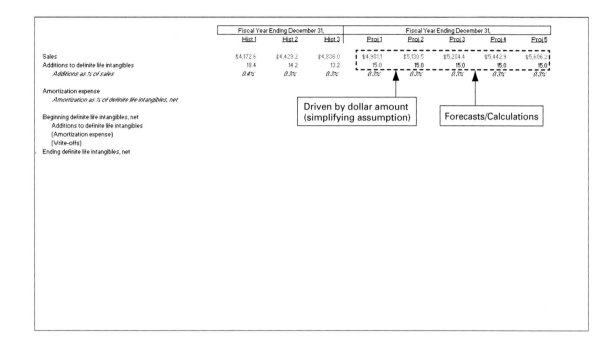

| | Fiscal Year Ending December 31, | | | Fiscal Year Ending December 31, | | | | |
	Hist 1	Hist 2	Hist 3	Proj 1	Proj 2	Proj 3	Proj 4	Proj 5
Sales	$4,172.6	$4,429.2	$4,806.0	$4,931.1	$5,130.5	$5,284.4	$5,442.9	$5,606.2
Additions to definite life intangibles	18.4	14.2	13.2	15.0	15.0	15.0	15.0	15.0
Additions as % of sales	*0.4%*	*0.3%*	*0.3%*	*0.3%*	*0.3%*	*0.3%*	*0.3%*	*0.3%*
Amortization expense								
Amortization as % of definite life intangibles, net								
Beginning definite life intangibles, net								
Additions to definite life intangibles								
(Amortization expense)								
(Write-offs)								
Ending definite life intangibles, net								

Driven by dollar amount (simplifying assumption)

Forecasts/Calculations

NOTES

There are a few resources you should consider when projecting additions to definite life intangibles:

- Go over historical financials; they often provide context for projections.
- Search the MD&A section of the company's most recent filing for management guidance.
  - Sometimes management communicates expected additions to definite life intangibles in this section.
- Use available research reports to 'sanity check' your assumptions.

Additions can be projected in two ways: (1) as a dollar amount or (2) based on additions as a percentage of sales.

- **As a dollar amount**: This is usually the better way if the company has historically spent the same amount every year, or if management provides specific numbers for how much they expect to spend.
- **As a percentage of sales**: This is generally the better method if additions to definite life intangibles have trended higher with increases in sales, or if management or research offers no guidance.

STEP 27

Reference historical information from the income statement and balance sheet

NOTES

	Fiscal Year Ending December 31,			Fiscal Year Ending December 31,				
	Hist 1	Hist 2	Hist 3	Proj 1	Proj 2	Proj 3	Proj 4	Proj 5
Sales	$4,172.6	$4,429.2	$4,836.0	$4,981.1	$5,130.5	$5,284.4	$5,442.9	$5,606.2
Additions to definite life intangibles	18.4	14.2	13.2	15.0	15.0	15.0	15.0	15.0
Additions as % of sales	*0.4%*	*0.3%*	*0.3%*	*0.3%*	*0.3%*	*0.3%*	*0.3%*	*0.3%*
Amortization expense	$21.8	$18.4	$17.9					
Amortization as % of definite life intangibles, net	*46.8%*	*30.2%*	*27.5%*					
Beginning definite life intangibles, net								
Additions to definite life intangibles			Historicals not needed					
(Amortization expense)								
(Write-offs)								
Ending definite life intangibles, net	$46.2	$61.0	$65.1					

References (GREEN) from income statement

Calculations

Will usually need a plug to reconcile; do not spend too much time doing this

References (GREEN) from balance sheet

Link historical amortization expense from the income statement.

Link historical definite life intangibles, net balance from the balance sheet. (We will deal with the indefinite life intangibles on the next schedule.)

- Focus on the ending balance for definite life intangibles, net. Don't worry about modeling the historical items that are used to reconcile this balance (for example, historical write-offs). It is typically difficult to reconcile historical definite life intangibles, net balances, because of a lack of information in the financial statements.

- If all intangibles are grouped together, or are included with goodwill, search for a goodwill and intangibles footnote in the financial statements for a breakout of these various balances.

Calculate amortization as a percentage of definite life intangibles, net.

NOTES

Project future amortization
expense

NOTES ....

....

....

....

....

....

....

	Fiscal Year Ending December 31,			Fiscal Year Ending December 31,				
	Hist 1	Hist 2	Hist 3	Proj 1	Proj 2	Proj 3	Proj 4	Proj 5
Sales	$4,172.6	$4,429.2	$4,836.0	$4,981.1	$5,130.5	$5,284.4	$5,442.9	$5,606.2
Additions to definite life intangibles	18.4	14.2	13.2	15.0	15.0	15.0	15.0	15.0
Additions as % of sales	*0.4%*	*0.3%*	*0.3%*	*0.3%*	*0.3%*	*0.3%*	*0.3%*	*0.3%*
Amortization expense	$21.6	$13.4	$17.9	$17.0	$16.5	$16.0	$15.5	$15.0
Amortization as % of definite life intangibles, net	*46.8%*	*30.2%*	*27.5%*					
Beginning definite life intangibles, net								
Additions to definite life intangibles								
(Amortization expense)								
(Write-offs)								
Ending definite life intangibles, net	$46.2	$61.0	$65.1					

Step ($0.5)

Forecast dollar amount based on management disclosure or historical numbers.

Use step to the right if needed to increase/(decrease) annual projections.

Search the financial footnotes of the company's most recent filing for information on future amortization expense. A company sometimes will provide guidance on this, though not always.

....

If the company does not provide projections, the straight-line method can be used to estimate amortization.

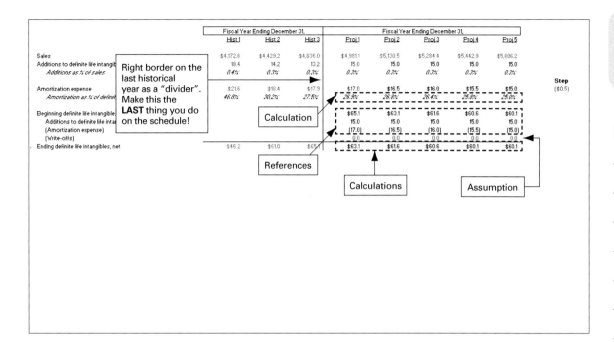

	Fiscal Year Ending December 31,			Fiscal Year Ending December 31,				
	Hist 1	Hist 2	Hist 3	Proj 1	Proj 2	Proj 3	Proj 4	Proj 5
Sales	$4,172.6	$4,429.2	$4,836.0	$4,981.1	$5,130.5	$5,284.4	$5,442.9	$5,606.2
Additions to definite life intangibles	18.4	14.2	13.2	15.0	15.0	15.0	15.0	15.0
Additions as % of sales	*0.4%*	*0.3%*	*0.3%*	*0.3%*	*0.3%*	*0.3%*	*0.3%*	*0.3%*
Amortization expense	$21.6	$18.4	$17.9	$17.0	$16.5	$16.0	$15.5	$15.0
Amortization as % of definite	*46.8%*	*30.2%*	*27.8%*	*26.9%*	*26.8%*	*26.4%*	*25.8%*	*25.0%*
Beginning definite life intangibles				$65.1	$63.1	$61.6	$60.6	$60.1
Additions to definite life intangibles				15.0	15.0	15.0	15.0	15.0
(Amortization expense)				(17.0)	(16.5)	(16.0)	(15.5)	(15.0)
(Write-offs)				0.0	0.0	0.0	0.0	0.0
Ending definite life intangibles, net	$48.2	$61.0	$65.1	$63.1	$61.6	$60.6	$60.1	$60.1

Step
($0.5)

Right border on the last historical year as a "divider". Make this the **LAST** thing you do on the schedule!

Calculation

References

Calculations

Assumption

The beginning definite life intangibles balance for one period is equal to the ending definite life intangibles balance for the previous year For example, the definite life intangibles balance on Proj 1 is the same as the definite life intangibles balance on Hist 3.

Reference additions to definite life intangibles from the projections you calculated in Step 26.

  – Additions are shown as <u>positive</u> here because, as a company makes additions, its definite life intangibles balance increases.

Reference amortization expense from the projections you calculated in Step 28.

  – Amortization is shown as <u>negative</u> here because as a company amortizes assets, its definite life intangibles balance decreases.

Make an assumption regarding future write-offs. If neither management nor research provides information, assume there are no write-offs.

  – Write-offs, if there are any, are shown as <u>negative</u> here because they decrease a company's definite life intangibles balance.

Calculate amortization as a percentage of definite life intangibles, net for the projected periods.

....

Link amortization projections to
the income statement

NOTES ....

	Fiscal Year Ending December 31,			Fiscal Year Ending December 31,				
	Hist 1	Hist 2	Hist 3	Proj 1	Proj 2	Proj 3	Proj 4	Proj 5
Sales	$4,172.6	$4,429.2	$4,836.0	$4,981.1	$5,130.5	$5,284.4	$5,442.9	$5,606.2
Cost of goods sold, excluding depreciation (1)	2,383.7	2,509.2	2,764.7	2,839.2	2,924.4	3,012.1	3,102.5	3,195.5
Gross profit	1,788.9	1,920.0	2,071.2	2,141.9	2,206.1	2,272.3	2,340.5	2,410.7
SG&A expenses, excluding amortization	819.5	848.7	895.1	896.6	923.5	951.2	979.7	1,009.1
Other operating (income) / expenses	0.0	0.0	0.0	0.0	0.0	0.0	0.0	0.0
EBITDA	969.4	1,071.4	1,176.1	1,245.3	1,282.6	1,321.1	1,360.7	1,401.6
Depreciation (1)	158.9	171.2	178.3	180.0	187.0	193.6	200.4	207.4
Amortization	21.6	18.4	17.9	17.0	16.5	16.0	15.5	15.0
EBIT (2)	788.8	881.7	979.9					
Interest expense	65.3	67.9	89.5					
Interest (income)	(1.7)	(1.4)	(1.5)					
Other non-operating (income) / expense	0.0	0.0	0.0		References			
Pretax income	725.3	815.2	891.9					
Income taxes (3)	266.2	298.4	324.7					
Net income (4)	**$459.1**	**$516.8**	**$567.3**					
Diluted weighted average shares in millions	264.532	256.934	248.292					
Earnings per share	**$1.74**	**$2.01**	**$2.28**					
Ratios & assumptions								
Sales growth rate		6.2%	9.2%	3.0%	3.0%	3.0%	3.0%	3.0%
Gross margin	42.9%	43.3%	42.8%	43.0%	43.0%	43.0%	43.0%	43.0%
SG&A expenses (as a % of sales)	19.6%	19.2%	18.5%	18.0%	18.0%	18.0%	18.0%	18.0%
Other operating (income) / expenses ($ amount)	$0.0	$0.0	$0.0	$0.0	$0.0	$0.0	$0.0	$0.0
Other non-operating (income) / expense ($ amount)	0.0	0.0	0.0					
Effective tax rate	36.7%	36.6%	36.4%					

Link projected amortization expense to the income statement.

– Make sure you are referencing from the correct years.

	Fiscal Year Ending December 31,			Fiscal Year Ending December 31,				
	Hist 1	Hist 2	Hist 3	Proj 1	Proj 2	Proj 3	Proj 4	Proj 5
Cash	$114.8	$54.8	$67.2					
Accounts receivable, net	407.6	408.9	559.3	573.2	590.4	608.1	626.3	645.1
Inventories	492.9	557.2	610.3	626.2	645.0	664.3	684.2	704.8
Other current assets	116.3	176.7	172.2	179.3	184.7	190.2	195.9	201.8
Total current assets	1,131.6	1,197.7	1,408.9					
PP&E, net	1,661.9	1,682.7	1,659.1	1,664.1	1,667.0	1,668.9	1,669.9	1,669.9
Definite life intangibles	46.2	61.0	65.1	63.1	61.6	60.6	60.1	60.1
Indefinite life intangibles	31.6	100.3	111.9					
Goodwill	389.0	463.9	487.3					
Other long-term assets	322.3	307.1	562.8					
Total assets	**$3,582.5**	**$3,812.8**	**$4,295.2**					
Accounts payable	$132.2	$148.7	$167.8	$171.1	$176.0	$181.6	$187.0	$192.8
Accrued liabilities	416.2	469.2	507.8	522.4	538.1	554.2	570.9	588.0
Other current liabilities	24.9	42.3	23.5	22.7	23.4	24.1	24.8	25.6
Total current liabilities	573.3	660.2	699.1					
Revolver	12.0	343.3	81.4					
Long-term debt	969.0	969.6	1,680.5					
Deferred income taxes	377.6	319.2	400.3					
Other long-term liabilities	370.8	383.4	412.9					
Total liabilities	2,302.7	2,675.7	3,274.2					
Total equity	1,279.9	1,137.1	1,021.1					
Total liabilities and equity	**$3,582.5**	**$3,812.8**	**$4,295.2**					
Parity check (A=L+E)	*0.000*	*0.000*	*0.000*					

References

STEP 31
....
Link definite life intangibles
projections to the balance sheet

NOTES ....

Link the projected <u>ending</u> *definite life intangibles, net* balance to the balance sheet.

   – Remember that the balance sheet represents values at one particular point in time; that is, the <u>last day</u> of the period (for example, Hist 3).

STEP 32

Link amortization and additions to intangibles projections to the cash flow statement

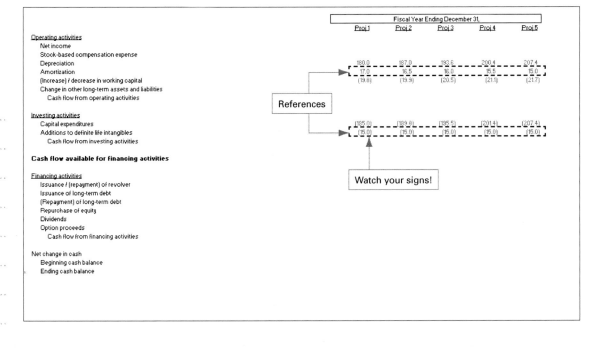

Link projected amortization expense to the cash flow statement. Be careful to link to the proper row—that is, toward the top of the sheet.

– Remember that amortization expense should be shown as <u>positive</u> here; it is being added back to net income as a non-cash expense.

Link projected additions to intangibles to the cash flow statement (look in the middle of the page, under investing activities).

– Remember that additions should be shown as <u>negative</u> here; they are cash outflows.

Flow-of-funds

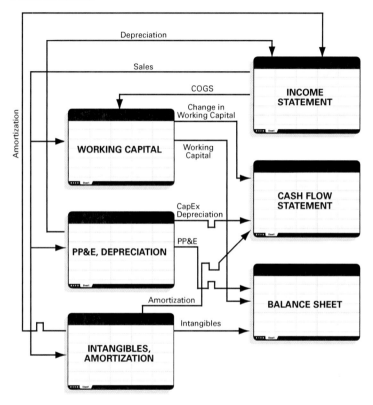

Stress Testing

After finishing the depreciation and amortization schedules, it is a good idea to check the signs of certain items both on the schedules themselves and on the cash flow statement where they are linked.

Go to your cash flow statement, and let's double-check the following:

1. Cash flow from operations

a. Depreciation should be shown as a <u>positive</u> number since it is a non-cash expense on the income statement and therefore added back to net income.

b. Amortization should be shown as a <u>positive</u> number since it is a non-cash expense on the income statement and therefore added back to net income.

2. Cash flow from investing activities

a. Capital expenditures should be shown as <u>negative</u> since they represent cash outflows.

b. Additions to intangibles should be shown as <u>negative</u> since they represent cash outflows.

Next, let's go to the balance sheet to make sure that items are correctly referenced. Go to the PP&E balance in the first projected year. Here we can apply a useful auditing technique for quickly checking cell references. If you hold down **Ctrl + [**, Excel will take you to the precedent cell (i.e., the cell that this cell is referencing). Once you have verified that the cell is referencing the ending balance of PP&E from the depreciation schedule, press **F5**, then press **enter** to go back to the balance sheet.

It is always important to check your core statements. Not only do you want to make sure that references are coming from the correct location, but you also want to double-check signs to adhere to the appropriate positive/negative sign convention.

 Please view the Online Companion for related supplementary media.

4.5 OTHER LONG-TERM ITEMS SCHEDULE

Ideally, a financial model would forecast every line item in detail. In practice, however, this would be quite challenging because some items do not have obvious drivers, or their future movements are difficult to anticipate.

Take, for example, a company's goodwill account, which reflects the premium the company has paid for past acquisitions. Goodwill could increase in the future if the company makes future acquisitions. Then again, goodwill could decrease if its value is impaired or written down. The uncertainty surrounding these future events makes it difficult to forecast this account.

Such characteristics make goodwill a great candidate for inclusion on the other long-term items schedule. The purpose of this schedule is to project long-term balance sheet items whose future balances are difficult to predict.

To set up this schedule, we first create the appropriate line items. We then reference historical balances for the long-term items. Because future movements in these balances are difficult to predict, we will keep them constant in projected periods. Next, we will calculate the cash flow impact of changes in these long-term items. Finally, we will link projected other long-term items balances back to the balance sheet and link their cash flow impact to the cash flow statement.

Other Long-Term Items Schedule for TTS Sample Company

Dollars in millions, except per share data

	Fiscal Year Ending December 31,			Fiscal Year Ending December 31,				
	Hist 1	Hist 2	Hist 3	Proj 1	Proj 2	Proj 3	Proj 4	Proj 5
Assets								
Indefinite life intangibles	$31.6	$100.3	$111.9					
Goodwill	389.0	463.9	487.3					
Other long-term assets	322.3	307.1	562.8					
Total other long-term assets	$742.8	$871.4	$1,162.1					
(Increase) / decrease in other long-term assets		*(128.6)*	*(290.7)*					
Liabilities								
Deferred income taxes	$377.6	$319.2	$400.3					
Other long-term liabilities	370.8	383.4	412.9					
Total other long-term liabilities	$748.4	$702.6	$813.2					
Increase / (decrease) in other long-term liabilities		*(45.8)*	*110.6*					
Change in other long-term assets and liabilities		**($174.3)**	**($180.1)**					

References (GREEN)

Calculations

References (GREEN)

Calculations

NOTES

Create line items for all the long-term assets and liabilities that do not have a clear driver or are otherwise difficult to predict (for example, other long-term assets/liabilities, goodwill, and deferred income taxes).

  – Notice that there is no relationship driver (for example, sales) at the top of the page.

Reference historical balances from the balance sheet.

Calculate totals for long-term assets and long-term liabilities.

Calculate the historical changes in total long-term assets and total long-term liabilities.

  – This line will eventually be linked to the cash flow statement, so be careful in your calculation.

   – Remember that increases in total long-term assets should be shown as negative because they represent a decrease in cash flow; decreases in total long-term assets should be shown as positive.

   – Conversely, increases in total long-term liabilities should be shown as positive and decreases should be shown as negative.

Calculate the total change in long-term assets and liabilities by adding together the change in total long-term assets and the change in total long-term liabilities.

STEP 34

Project future balances

NOTES

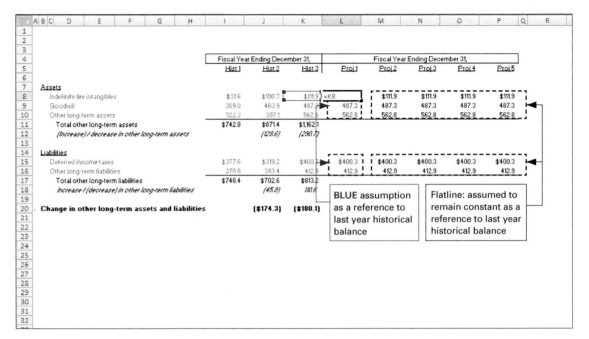

		Fiscal Year Ending December 31,			Fiscal Year Ending December 31,				
		Hist 1	Hist 2	Hist 3	Proj 1	Proj 2	Proj 3	Proj 4	Proj 5
Assets									
Indefinite life intangibles		$31.6	$100.3	$111.9	=K8	$111.9	$111.9	$111.9	$111.9
Goodwill		389.0	463.9	487.2	487.3	487.3	487.3	487.3	487.3
Other long-term assets		322.3	307.1	562.8	562.8	562.8	562.8	562.8	562.8
Total other long-term assets		$742.8	$871.4	$1,162.1					
(Increase) / decrease in other long-term assets			(128.6)	(290.7)					
Liabilities									
Deferred income taxes		$377.6	$319.2	$400.2	$400.3	$400.3	$400.3	$400.3	$400.3
Other long-term liabilities		370.8	383.4	412.9	412.9	412.9	412.9	412.9	412.9
Total other long-term liabilities		$748.4	$702.6	$813.2					
Increase / (decrease) in other long-term liabilities			(45.8)	110.6					
Change in other long-term assets and liabilities			**($174.3)**	**($180.1)**					

BLUE assumption as a reference to last year historical balance

Flatline: assumed to remain constant as a reference to last year historical balance

Choose a method for projecting future balances based on what you know about the target company and its industry. Research reports can be a useful guide here.

Consider keeping balances constant if there is no obvious driver or if guidance from management or research is unavailable. Remember the modeling mantra: assumptions should be "reasonable and defensible." When information is scarce, be conservative in your approach.

– The balance in the first projected year should reference the balance in the last historical year. This will keep the balance exactly the same, thereby not affecting cash flow. Format this cell blue.

– But shouldn't this cell be black, you might ask. Aren't we breaking a color scheme best practice? True, this cell is a reference to another cell (rather than an input) so technically it should be black. We nevertheless recommend making this cell blue to serve as a reminder that an assumption was made here.

– Flatline the $ amount of the remaining projected years; these cells are formulas and should be black.

 Please view the Online Companion for related supplementary media.

Calculate the projected totals and change in cash flows

	Fiscal Year Ending December 31,			Fiscal Year Ending December 31,				
	Hist 1	Hist 2	Hist 3	Proj 1	Proj 2	Proj 3	Proj 4	Proj 5
Assets								
Indefinite life intangibles	$31.6	$100.3	$111.9	$111.9	$111.9	$111.9	$111.9	$111.9
Goodwill	393.0	463.9	487.0	487.3	487.3	487.3	487.3	487.3
Other long-term assets	322.3	307.1	562.8	562.8	562.8	562.8	562.8	562.8
Total other long-term asse	$742.8	$871.4	$1,162.1	$1,162.1	$1,162.1	$1,162.1	$1,162.1	$1,162.1
(Increase)/decrease in o		*(128.6)*	*(290.7)*	*0.0*	*0.0*	*0.0*	*0.0*	*0.0*
Liabilities								
Deferred income taxes	$377.6	$319.2	$400.3	$400.3	$400.3	$400.3	$400.3	$400.3
Other long-term liabilities	370.8	383.4	412.9	412.9	412.9	412.9	412.9	412.9
Total other long-term liabilities	$748.4	$702.6	$813.2	$813.2	$813.2	$813.2	$813.2	$813.2
Increase/(decrease) in other long-term liabilities		*(45.8)*	*110.6*	*0.0*	*0.0*	*0.0*	*0.0*	*0.0*
Change in other long-term assets and liabilities		**($174.3)**	**($180.1)**	**$0.0**	**$0.0**	**$0.0**	**$0.0**	**$0.0**

Right border on the last historical year as a "divider". Make this the **LAST** thing you do on the schedule!

Calculations

NOTES

Calculate the projected total long-term assets and total long-term liabilities.

Calculate the projected decrease/(increase) in total long-term assets and the increase/(decrease) in total long-term liabilities.

– Remember the rules from Step 33: increases in total long-term assets should be negative (cash outflows); increases in total long-term liabilities should be positive (cash inflows).

– Be efficient wherever possible. If you built the formulas in Step 33 properly, you should be able to copy and paste those formulas for the projected periods.

Calculate the total change in other long-term assets and liabilities.

Take a step back and check your results. If you held each of the balances constant, then the changes calculated in the projected years should be zero (as shown above). Remember, we are calculating a zero (or 'neutral') cash impact from changes in other long-term assets and liabilities.

NOTES

	Fiscal Year Ending December 31,			Fiscal Year Ending December 31,				
	Hist 1	Hist 2	Hist 3	Proj 1	Proj 2	Proj 3	Proj 4	Proj 5
Cash	$114.8	$54.8	$67.2					
Accounts receivable, net	407.6	408.9	559.3	573.2	590.4	608.1	626.3	645.1
Inventories	492.9	557.2	610.3	626.2	645.0	664.3	684.2	704.8
Other current assets	116.3	176.7	172.2	179.3	184.7	190.2	195.9	201.8
Total current assets	1,131.6	1,197.7	1,408.9					
PP&E, net	1,661.9	1,682.7	1,659.1	1,664.1	1,667.0	1,668.9	1,669.9	1,669.9
Definite life intangibles	46.2	61.0	65.1	63.1	61.6	60.6	60.1	60.1
Indefinite life intangibles	31.6	100.3	111.9	111.9	111.9	111.9	111.9	111.9
Goodwill	389.0	463.9	487.3	487.3	487.3	487.3	487.3	487.3
Other long-term assets	322.3	307.1	562.8	562.8	562.8	562.8	562.8	562.8
Total assets	**$3,582.5**	**$3,812.8**	**$4,295.2**					
Accounts payable	$132.2	$148.7	$167.8	$171.1	$176.3	$181.6	$187.0	$192.6
Accrued liabilities	416.2	469.2	507.8	522.4	538.1	554.2	570.9	588.0
Other current liabilities	24.9	42.3	23.5	22.7	23.4	24.1	24.8	25.6
Total current liabilities	573.3	660.2	699.1					
Revolver	12.0	343.3	81.4					
Long-term debt	969.0	969.6	1,680.5					
Deferred income taxes	377.6	319.2	400.3	400.3	400.3	400.3	400.3	400.3
Other long-term liabilities	370.8	383.4	412.9	412.9	412.9	412.9	412.9	412.9
Total liabilities	2,302.7	2,675.7	3,274.2					
Total equity	1,279.9	1,137.1	1,021.1					
Total liabilities and equity	**$3,582.5**	**$3,812.8**	**$4,295.2**					
Parity check (A=L+E)	0.000	0.000	0.000					

References (GREEN)

Link projected other long-term assets and other long-term liabilities balances to the balance sheet.

– Make sure links between worksheets reference the correct line items.

– Make sure links between worksheets reference the correct years (for example, Proj1 balances on the balance sheet should reference Proj1 balances on the other long-term items schedule).

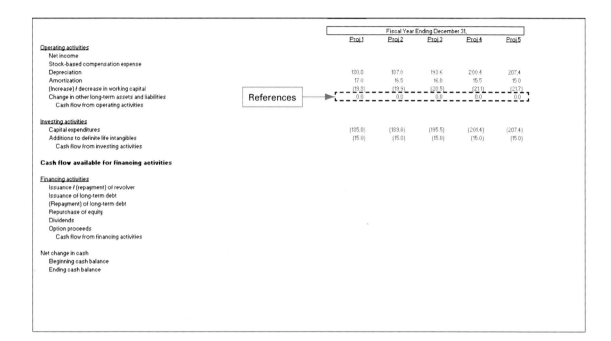

	Fiscal Year Ending December 31,				
	Proj 1	Proj 2	Proj 3	Proj 4	Proj 5
Operating activities					
Net income					
Stock-based compensation expense					
Depreciation	180.0	187.0	193.6	200.4	207.4
Amortization	17.0	16.5	16.0	15.5	15.0
(Increase) / decrease in working capital	(19.3)	(19.9)	(20.5)	(21.1)	(21.7)
Change in other long-term assets and liabilities	0.0	0.0	0.0	0.0	0.0
Cash flow from operating activities					
Investing activities					
Capital expenditures	(185.0)	(189.8)	(195.5)	(201.4)	(207.4)
Additions to definite life intangibles	(15.0)	(15.0)	(15.0)	(15.0)	(15.0)
Cash flow from investing activities					
Cash flow available for financing activities					
Financing activities					
Issuance / (repayment) of revolver					
Issuance of long-term debt					
(Repayment) of long-term debt					
Repurchase of equity					
Dividends					
Option proceeds					
Cash flow from financing activities					
Net change in cash					
Beginning cash balance					
Ending cash balance					

References

Link the projected change in total long-term assets and liabilities to its corresponding line item on the cash flow statement.

– If you set up the formulas correctly, the calculated change should accurately reflect the cash impact of the change in other long-term assets and liabilities. In the above example, the cash flow impact is zero.

Flow-of-funds

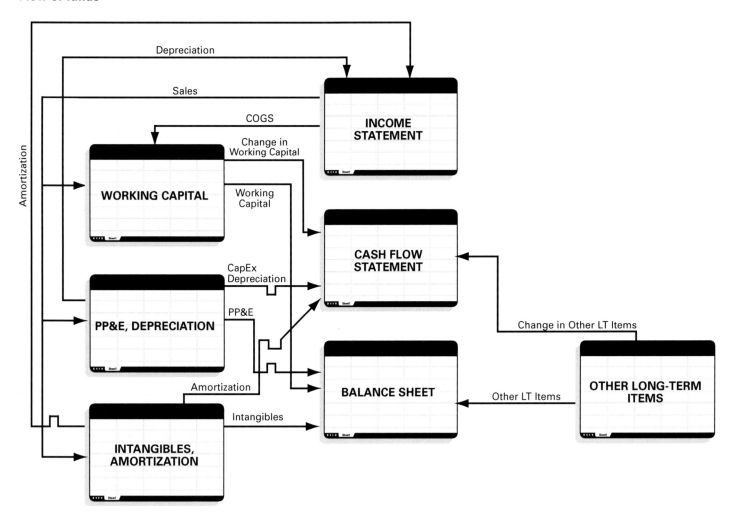

Notice that in this illustration of flow-of-funds, there are no relationship drivers flowing into the other long-term items schedule.

Stress Testing

Let's stress-test the other long-term items schedule to ensure that projected cash flow impacts are flowing properly.

Go to the first projected year of any long-term asset account. Input an increase in the asset and ask: Does the cash flow become negative in the first year? If not, double-check the cash flow line and verify that changes in other long-term assets have been calculated properly.

Now, go to the first projected year of any long-term liability account. Input an increase in the liability and ask: Does the cash flow become positive in the first year? If not, double-check the cash flow line and verify that changes in other long-term liabilities have been calculated properly.

Once you are satisfied that projected cash flow impacts are flowing properly, revert back to the original flatline formulas created in step 34.

 Please view the Online Companion for related supplementary media.

4.6 COMPLETING THE INCOME STATEMENT LOGIC

When building a model, you sometimes need to finish the formulas and calculations on one worksheet before starting another one. In this section, we will forecast certain income statement items (but not interest expense and interest income) in order to calculate projected earnings per share. Why do we need to do this? Because in the next supporting schedule (shareholders' equity), we will use projected earnings per share to imply the prices at which the company can buy back its own shares.

In this section, we will make shares outstanding in projected years equal to shares outstanding in the last historical year. This is just a temporary action designed to generate earnings per share values. Later, shares outstanding will be projected on the shares outstanding schedule. One other thing: Note that, for now, we are leaving that projected interest expense/(income) blank. It will be projected later on the debt and interest schedule.

We will also finish calculating the various ratios and formulas on the income statement, including the **compounded annual growth rate (CAGR)** for key income statement line items. Note that our aim here is simply to build the mechanics, or "logic," of these key calculations. Similar to our 'temporary' shares outstanding projections, these values will change as we complete the final steps of our model.

Project shares outstanding on
the income statement

NOTES ....

	Fiscal Year Ending December 31,			Fiscal Year Ending December 31,				
	Hist 1	Hist 2	Hist 3	Proj 1	Proj 2	Proj 3	Proj 4	Proj 5
Sales	$4,172.6	$4,429.2	$4,836.0	$4,981.1	$5,130.5	$5,284.4	$5,442.9	$5,606.2
Cost of goods sold, excluding depreciation (1)	2,383.7	2,509.2	2,764.7	2,839.2	2,924.4	3,012.1	3,102.5	3,195.5
Gross profit	1,788.9	1,920.0	2,071.2	2,141.9	2,206.1	2,272.3	2,340.5	2,410.7
SG&A expenses, excluding amortization	819.5	848.7	895.1	896.6	923.5	951.2	979.7	1,009.1
Other operating (income) / expenses	0.0	0.0	0.0	0.0	0.0	0.0	0.0	0.0
EBITDA	969.4	1,071.4	1,176.1	1,245.3	1,282.6	1,321.1	1,360.7	1,401.6
Depreciation (1)	158.9	171.2	178.3	180.0	187.0	193.6	200.4	207.4
Amortization	21.6	18.4	17.9	17.0	16.5	16.0	15.5	15.0
EBIT (2)	788.8	881.7	979.9					
Interest expense	65.3	67.9	89.5					
Interest (income)	(1.7)	(1.4)	(1.5)					
Other non-operating (income) / expense	0.0	0.0	0.0					
Pretax income	725.3	815.2	891.9					
Income taxes (3)	266.2	298.4	324.7					
Net income (4)	**$459.1**	**$516.8**	**$567.3**					
Diluted weighted average shares in millions	264.532	256.934	248.292	248.292	248.292	248.292	248.292	248.292
Earnings per share	**$1.74**	**$2.01**	**$2.28**					
Ratios & assumptions								
Sales growth rate		6.2%	9.2%	3.0%	3.0%	3.0%	3.0%	3.0%
Gross margin	42.9%	43.3%	42.8%	43.0%	43.0%	43.0%	43.0%	43.0%
SG&A expenses (as a % of sales)	19.6%	19.2%	18.5%	18.0%	18.0%	18.0%	18.0%	18.0%
Other operating (income) / expenses ($ amount)	$0.0	$0.0	$0.0	$0.0	$0.0	$0.0	$0.0	$0.0
Other non-operating (income) / expense ($ amount)	0.0	0.0	0.0					
Effective tax rate	36.7%	36.6%	36.4%					

Keep constant
[will change later]

Consider making
RED as reminder

Use a flatline to make projected shares outstanding balances equal to the last historical period.

– We will revisit this after completing the shareholders' equity and shares outstanding schedules.

– Consider making these cells red to indicate that they should be revisited later.

	Fiscal Year Ending December 31,			Fiscal Year Ending December 31,				
	Hist 1	Hist 2	Hist 3	Proj 1	Proj 2	Proj 3	Proj 4	Proj 5
Sales	$4,172.6	$4,429.2	$4,836.0	$4,981.1	$5,130.5	$5,284.4	$5,442.9	$5,606.2
Cost of goods sold, excluding depreciation (1)	2,383.7	2,509.2	2,764.7	2,839.2	2,924.4	3,012.1	3,102.5	3,195.5
Gross profit	1,788.9	1,920.0	2,071.2	2,141.9	2,206.1	2,272.3	2,340.5	2,410.7
SG&A expenses, excluding amortization	819.5	848.7	895.1	896.6	923.5	951.2	979.7	1,009.1
Other operating (income) / expenses	0.0	0.0	0.0	0.0	0.0	0.0	0.0	0.0
EBITDA	969.4	1,071.4	1,176.1	1,245.3	1,282.6	1,321.1	1,360.7	1,401.6
Depreciation (1)	158.9	171.2	178.3	180.0	197.0	193.8	200.4	207.4
Amortization	21.6	18.4	17.9	17.0	16.5	16.0	15.5	15.0
EBIT (2)	788.8	881.7	979.9	1,048.3	1,079.1	1,111.5	1,144.9	1,179.1
Interest expense	65.3	67.9	89.5					
Interest (income)	(1.7)	(1.4)	(1.5)					
Other non-operating (income) / expense	0.0	0.0	0.0					
Pretax income	725.3	815.2	891.9	1,048.3	1,079.1	1,111.5	1,144.9	1,179.1
Income taxes (3)	266.2	298.4	324.7					
Net income (4)	**$459.1**	**$516.8**	**$567.2**	**$1,048.3**	**$1,079.1**	**$1,111.5**	**$1,144.9**	**$1,179.1**
Diluted weighted average shares in millions	264.532	256.934	248.292	248.292	248.292	248.292	248.292	248.292
Earnings per share	**$1.74**	**$2.01**	**$2.29**	**$4.22**	**$4.35**	**$4.48**	**$4.61**	**$4.75**
Ratios & assumptions								
Sales growth rate		6.2%	9.2%	3.0%	3.0%	3.0%	3.0%	3.0%
Gross margin	42.9%	43.3%	42.8%	43.0%	43.0%	43.0%	43.0%	43.0%
SG&A expenses (as a % of sales)	19.6%	19.2%	18.5%	18.0%	18.0%	18.0%	18.0%	18.0%
Other operating (income) / expenses ($ amount)	$0.0	$0.0	$0.0	$0.0	$0.0	$0.0	$0.0	$0.0
Other non-operating (income) / expense ($ amount)	0.0	0.0	0.0					
Effective tax rate	36.7%	36.6%	36.4%					

Calculations

Calculate EBIT, pre-tax income, net income, and EPS for the projected years.

 – Leave interest expense, interest income, other non-operating income/expense, and taxes blank for now.

 – Again, be efficient! Fill right the historical formulas across the projected periods.

 Please view the Online Companion for related supplementary media.

STEP 40

Project non-operating income/
expense and calculate taxes

NOTES

	Fiscal Year Ending December 31,			Fiscal Year Ending December 31,				
	Hist 1	Hist 2	Hist 3	Proj 1	Proj 2	Proj 3	Proj 4	Proj 5
Sales	$4,172.6	$4,429.2	$4,836.0	$4,981.1	$5,130.5	$5,284.4	$5,442.9	$5,606.2
Cost of goods sold, excluding depreciation (1)	2,383.7	2,509.2	2,764.7	2,839.2	2,924.4	3,012.1	3,102.5	3,195.5
Gross profit	1,788.9	1,920.0	2,071.2	2,141.9	2,206.1	2,272.3	2,340.5	2,410.7
SG&A expenses, excluding amortization	819.5	848.7	895.1	896.6	923.5	951.2	979.7	1,009.1
Other operating (income) / expenses	0.0	0.0	0.0	0.0	0.0	0.0	0.0	0.0
EBITDA	969.4	1,071.4	1,176.1	1,245.3	1,282.6	1,321.1	1,360.7	1,401.6
Depreciation (1)	158.9	171.2	178.3	180.0	187.0	193.6	200.4	207.4
Amortization	21.6	18.4	17.9	17.0	16.5	16.0	15.5	15.0
EBIT (2)	788.8	881.7	979.9	1,048.3	1,079.1	1,111.5	1,144.9	1,179.1
Interest expense	65.3	67.9	89.5					
Interest (income)	(1.7)	(1.4)	(1.5)					Reference
Other non-operating (income) / expense	0.0	0.0	0.0	0.0	0.0	0.0	0.0	0.0
Pretax income	725.3	815.2	891.9	1,048.3	1,079.1	1,111.5	1,144.9	1,179.1
Income taxes (3)	266.2	298.4	324.7	379.5	390.6	402.4	414.4	426.8
Net income (4)	**$459.1**	**$516.8**	**$567.3**	**$668.8**	**$688.5**	**$709.2**	**$730.4**	**$752.3**
Diluted weighted average shares in millions	264.532	256.934	248.292	248.292	248.292	248.292	24 Calculations	
Earnings per share	**$1.74**	**$2.01**	**$2.28**	**$2.69**	**$2.77**	**$2.86**	**$2.94**	**$3.03**
Ratios & assumptions				Drivers				
Sales growth rate		6.2%		3.0%	3.0%	3.0%	3.0%	3.0%
Gross margin	42.9%	43.3%	42.8%	43.0%	43.0%	43.0%	43.0%	43.0%
SG&A expenses (as a % of sales)	19.6%	19.2%	18.5%	18.0%	18.0%	18.0%	18.0%	18.0%
Other operating (income) / expenses ($ amount)	$0.0	$0.0	$0.0	$0.0	$0.0	$0.0	$0.0	$0.0
Other non-operating (income) / expense ($ amount)	0.0	0.0	0.0	0.0	0.0	0.0	0.0	0.0
Effective tax rate	36.7%	36.6%	36.4%	36.2%	36.2%	36.2%	36.2%	36.2%

Project non-operating income/expense based on historical data.

– If no other information is available, make an assumption based on historical numbers and hold it constant.

Choose a reasonable tax rate for the first projected period based on historical data. Keep this assumption constant in subsequent periods, or use a step function to raise or lower it slightly.

Use your assumed tax rate to calculate projected taxes.

Leave interest expense and interest income blank for now. We will link these in after completing the debt and interest schedule.

Calculate the compounded annual growth rates (CAGRs) for the most important items. These typically include: sales, gross profit, EBITDA, EBIT, net income, and EPS.

– The CAGRs should be calculated by taking the most recent historical period and comparing it to the last year of projections.

– The formula for the CAGR is:

 $$\left(\frac{FV}{PV} \right)^{1/N} - 1$$

In this formula, FV represents the future value, PV represents the present value, and N represents the number of periods.

– To calculate the CAGR, you can use either the formula above or use the RATE function in Excel.

– Nper – The number of periods. In our example, there are five years between Hist 3 and Proj 5.

– Pmt – The amount of annual payments being made, if any. Ignore this for now and input zero.

– Pv – The present value amount. In our example, this would be sales in Hist 3. It's important to remember that this number needs to be negative.

– Fv – The future value amount. In our example, this would be sales in Proj 5.

– Type – Ignore this for now and leave blank.

Reference the Microsoft Excel Help guide for a more detailed description of the RATE function.

REFER TO SCREENSHOT ON THE RIGHT ⟶

 Please view the Online Companion for related supplementary media.

	Fiscal Year Ending December 31,			Fiscal Year Ending December 31,					5 Year CAGR
	Hist 1	Hist 2	Hist 3	Proj 1	Proj 2	Proj 3	Proj 4	Proj 5	
Sales	$4,172.6	$4,429.2	$4,836.0	$4,981.1	$5,130.5	$5,284.4	$5,442.9	$5,606.2	3.0%
Cost of goods sold, excluding depreciation (1)	2,383.7	2,509.2	2,764.7	2,839.2	2,924.4	3,012.1	3,102.5	3,195.5	
Gross profit	1,788.9	1,920.0	2,071.2	2,141.9	2,206.1	2,272.3	2,340.5	2,410.7	3.1%
SG&A expenses, excluding amortization	819.5	848.7	895.1	896.6	923.5	951.2	979.7	1,009.1	
Other operating (income) / expenses	0.0	0.0	0.0	0.0	0.0	0.0	0.0	0.0	
EBITDA	969.4	1,071.4	1,176.1	1,245.3	1,282.6	1,321.1	1,360.7	1,401.6	3.6%
Depreciation (1)	158.9	171.2	178.3	180.0	197.0	193.6	200.4	207.4	
Amortization	21.6	18.4	17.9	17.0	16.5	16.0	15.5	15.0	
EBIT (2)	788.8	881.7	979.9	1,048.3	1,079.1	1,111.5	1,144.9	1,179.1	3.8%
Interest expense	65.3	67.9	89.5						
Interest (income)	(1.7)	(1.4)	(1.5)						
Other non-operating (income) / expense	0.0	0.0	0.0	0.0	0.0	0.0	0.0	0.0	
Pretax income	725.3	815.2	891.9	1,048.3	1,079.1	1,111.5	1,144.9	1,179.1	5.7%
Income taxes (3)	266.2	298.4	324.7	379.5	390.6	402.4	414.4	426.8	
Net income (4)	**$459.1**	**$516.8**	**$567.3**	**$668.8**	**$688.5**	**$709.2**	**$730.4**	**$752.3**	**5.8%**
Diluted weighted average shares in millions	264.532	256.934	248.292	248.292	248.292	248.292	248.292	248.292	0.0%
Earnings per share	**$1.74**	**$2.01**	**$2.28**	**$2.69**	**$2.77**	**$2.86**	**$2.94**	**$3.03**	**5.8%**
Ratios & assumptions									
Sales growth rate		6.2%	9.2%	3.0%	3.0%	3.0%	3.0%	3.0%	
Gross margin	42.9%	43.3%	42.8%	43.0%	43.0%	43.0%	43.0%	43.0%	
SG&A expenses (as a % of sales)	19.6%	19.2%	18.5%	18.0%	18.0%	18.0%	18.0%	18.0%	
Other operating (income) / expenses ($ amount)	$0.0	$0.0	$0.0	$0.0	$0.0	$0.0	$0.0	$0.0	
Other non-operating (income) / expense ($ amount)	0.0	0.0	0.0	0.0	0.0	0.0	0.0	0.0	
Effective tax rate	36.7%	36.6%	36.4%	36.2%	36.2%	36.2%	36.2%	36.2%	

Calculate the relevant CAGRS

Use the RATE formula. Watch your signs on the PV and FV.

NOTES

4.7 SHAREHOLDERS' EQUITY SCHEDULE

This schedule represents a turning point in the model. So far, we have focused on modeling operating assets and liabilities. We have yet to discuss the capital sources of the firm: its equity and debt holders. In this schedule, we will focus on the equity holders by forecasting shareholders' equity.

If you look at shareholder's equity as reported on a typical company's balance sheet, you will likely see some of the following items (possibly under different names):

- Additional paid in capital
- Par value
- Retained earnings/loss

Since our model is more concerned with cash flow impacts than it is with accounting categorizations, our shareholders' equity schedule will focus on aggregate accounts. For example, if a company were to raise fresh equity capital, then it would record increases in both its additional paid in capital and par value accounts. By contrast, here we will combine the two accounts, reflecting an increase in the aggregate equity account.

We will also project three corporate actions that typically affect shareholders:

- Share repurchases
- Option proceeds and new shares issued for exercised options
- Dividends

After we build and forecast the line items on this schedule, we will link their ending balances to the balance sheet. We will also link changes in share repurchases, options, and dividends to the cash flow statement.

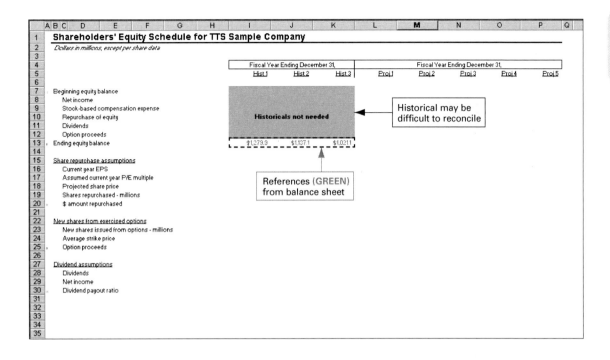

Set up the line items as shown.

Reference ending shareholders' equity from the balance sheet for historical periods.

Add lines for other equity-related items that are relevant, such as options, share repurchases, or dividends.

– Not all of these may be relevant for all companies because not all companies issue options to employees, buy back shares, or pay dividends to shareholders. Read through the MD&A and footnotes in the company's latest filing to determine which items are relevant to the company you are modeling.

NOTES . . . .

	Fiscal Year Ending December 31,			Fiscal Year Ending December 31,				
	Hist 1	Hist 2	Hist 3	Proj 1	Proj 2	Proj 3	Proj 4	Proj 5
Beginning equity balance								
Net income								
Stock-based compensation expense								
Repurchase of equity								
Dividends								
Option proceeds								
Ending equity balance	$1,279.9	$1,137.1	$1,021.1					
Share repurchase assumptions								
Current year EPS								
Assumed current year P/E multiple								
Projected share price								
Shares repurchased - millions	12.259	15.813	9.013					
$ amount repurchased	$414.8	$698.9	$537.0					
New shares from exercised options								
New shares issued from options - millions								
Average strike price								
Option proceeds								
Dividend assumptions								
Dividends								
Net income								
Dividend payout ratio								

BLUE inputs

Input the historical data for share repurchases, if any.

  – In this step, you need to find:

    1. The number of shares the company repurchased

    2. The $ amount the company spent on share repurchases.

Data can be found in the company filings or company-provided financial reports. Look for the relevant data either in the financial footnotes, on the cash flow statement, or on the shareholders' equity schedule.

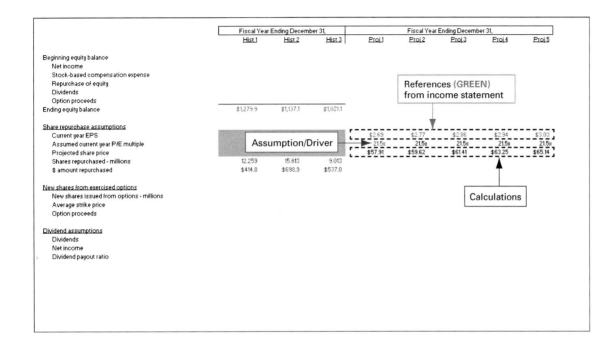

Reference projected earnings per share from the income statement.

Choose a reasonable and defensible P/E multiple stock (price divided by earnings per share) for the first projected period.

- Calculate the current trading P/E multiple. Spread the public comparables to get a sense of where the company 'should' trade. Please refer to our corporate valuation self-study package for more information regarding public comparables analysis.

- Consult research to get a 'consensus' view of where the company is expected to trade in the future.

- You can keep this P/E multiple constant over the projected periods, or use a step function to increase or decrease it slightly over time.

Calculate the projected share price by multiplying the projected EPS by the assumed P/E multiple. This will provide a projected share price for the company.

STEP 45

Calculate the dollar amount of shares repurchased

NOTES

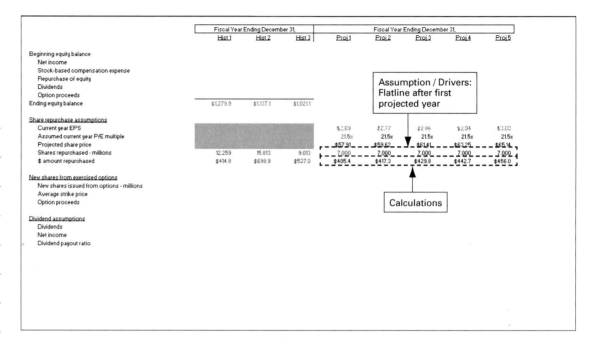

Make a reasonable assumption (blue cell) for number of shares repurchased.

– Look at historical repurchases, research reports, and information in the news about the company's announced share repurchase program.

– Be careful! Make sure you input numbers in a consistent format. If dollar amounts have been inputted in millions, then shares should also be inputted in millions.

Calculate the projected $ amount by multiplying the number of shares repurchased by the projected share price.

	Fiscal Year Ending December 31,			Fiscal Year Ending December 31,				
	Hist 1	Hist 2	Hist 3	Proj 1	Proj 2	Proj 3	Proj 4	Proj 5
Beginning equity balance								
Net income								
Stock-based compensation expense								
Repurchase of equity								
Dividends								
Option proceeds								
Ending equity balance	$1,279.9	$1,137.1	$1,021.1					
Share repurchase assumptions								
Current year EPS				$2.69	$2.77	$2.86	$2.94	$3.03
Assumed current year P/E multiple				21.5x	21.5x	21.5x	21.5x	21.5x
Projected share price				$57.91	$59.62	$61.41	$63.25	$65.14
Shares repurchased - millions	12.259	15.813	9.013	7.000	7.000	7.000	7.000	7.000
$ amount repurchased	$414.8	$698.3	$537.0	$405.4	$417.3	$429.8	$442.7	$456.0
New shares from exercised options								
New shares issued from options - millions	2.878	3.341	2.949					
Average strike price								
Option proceeds	$69.3	$104.7	$122.7					
Dividend assumptions								
Dividends								
Net income								
Dividend payout ratio								

BLUE inputs

Input the historical data for new shares issued from options and option proceeds.

– In this step, you need to find:

1. The number of new shares that were issued as a result of options that were exercised.

2. The $ amount the company received when the option holders exercised their shares. This results in a net cash inflow for the company. Please refer to our corporate valuation self-study package for more information regarding options and option proceeds.

– Look for the historical data in company-provided financial reports, or in the statement of shareholders' equity, or financial footnotes of the company's filings.

STEP 47

Calculate option proceeds

	Fiscal Year Ending December 31,			Fiscal Year Ending December 31,				
	Hist 1	Hist 2	Hist 3	Proj 1	Proj 2	Proj 3	Proj 4	Proj 5
Beginning equity balance								
Net income								
Stock-based compensation expense								
Repurchase of equity								
Dividends								
Option proceeds								
Ending equity balance	$1,279.9	$1,137.1	$1,021.1					
Share repurchase assumptions								
Current year EPS				$2.69	$2.77	$2.86	$2.94	$0.00
Assumed current year P/E multiple				21.5x	21.5x	21.5x	21.5x	21.5x
Projected share price				$57.91	$59.62	$61.41	$63.25	$65.14
Shares repurchased - millions	12.259	15.813	9.013	7.000	7.000	7.000	7.000	7.000
$ amount repurchased	$414.8	$698.9	$537.0	$405.4	$417.3	$429.8	$442.7	$456.0
New shares from exercised options								
New shares issued from options - millions	2.878	3.341	2.949	3.000	3.000	3.000	3.000	3.000
Average strike price				$30.86	$30.86	$30.86	$30.86	$30.86
Option proceeds	$69.3	$104.7	$122.7	$92.6	$92.6	$92.6	$92.6	$92.6
Dividend assumptions								
Dividends								
Net income								
Dividend payout ratio								

Assumption/Driver

Calculations

Create a reasonable assumption for the number of new shares to be issued from options based on the historical data.

– Either hold this number constant in all projected periods, or assume a continuing trend based on historical data.

Create a reasonable assumption for an average strike price per option.

– This assumption could be based on historical data or based on the current share price.

– You can also look at the footnotes in a company filing for strike price information about most recent outstanding/exercisable options.

Calculate the total option proceeds in dollars by multiplying the average strike price and the number of new shares to be issued from options. (This results in a cash inflow to the company.)

Alternatively, you could assume a total dollar amount for proceeds from options.

	Fiscal Year Ending December 31,			Fiscal Year Ending December 31,				
	Hist 1	Hist 2	Hist 3	Proj 1	Proj 2	Proj 3	Proj 4	Proj 5
Beginning equity balance								
Net income								
Stock-based compensation expense								
Repurchase of equity								
Dividends								
Option proceeds								
Ending equity balance	$1,279.9	$1,137.1	$1,021.1					
Share repurchase assumptions								
Current year EPS				$2.69	$2.77	$2.86	$2.94	$3.03
Assumed current year P/E multiple				21.5x	21.5x	21.5x	21.5x	21.5x
Projected share price				$57.91	$59.62	$61.41	$63.25	$65.14
Shares repurchased - millions	12.259	15.813	9.013	7.000	7.000	7.000	7.000	7.000
$ amount repurchased	$414.8	$698.3	$537.0	$405.4	$417.3	$429.8	$442.7	$456.0
New shares from exercised options								
New shares issued from options - millions	2.878	3.341	2.949	3.000	3.000	3.000	3.000	3.000
Average strike price				$30.86	$30.86	$30.86	$30.86	$30.86
Option proceeds	$69.3	$104.7	$122.7	$92.6	$92.6	$92.6	$92.6	$92.6
Dividend assumptions								
Dividends	$184.7	$205.7	$221.2					
Net income	459.1	516.9	567.1					
Dividend payout ratio	40.2%	39.8%	39.0%					

BLUE inputs

BLACK calculations

References (GREEN) from income statement

Look for the historical dividend data in company-provided financial reports, or in the MD&A or financial footnotes of the company's filings.

– The cash flow statement (under cash flows from financing activities) is a good starting point.

Input the historical amount of total dividends paid in dollars.

Reference in historical net income from the income statement.

Calculate the historical dividend payout ratio by dividing total dividends paid by net income:

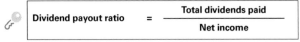

$$\text{Dividend payout ratio} = \frac{\text{Total dividends paid}}{\text{Net income}}$$

Additionally, you may consider inputting a line item for dividends paid per share. This is a common metric examined by analysts and investors.

NOTES

	Fiscal Year Ending December 31,			Fiscal Year Ending December 31,				
	Hist 1	Hist 2	Hist 3	Proj 1	Proj 2	Proj 3	Proj 4	Proj 5
Beginning equity balance								
Net income								
Stock-based compensation expense								
Repurchase of equity								
Dividends								
Option proceeds								
Ending equity balance	$1,279.9	$1,137.1	$1,021.1					
Share repurchase assumptions								
Current year EPS				$2.69	$2.77	$2.86	$2.94	$3.00
Assumed current year P/E multiple				21.5x	21.5x	21.5x	21.5x	21.5x
Projected share price				$57.91	$59.62	$61.41	$63.25	$65.14
Shares repurchased - millions	12.259	15.813	9.013	7.000	7.000	7.000	7.000	7.000
$ amount repurchased	$414.8	$698.9	$537.0	$405.4	$417.3	$429.8	$442.7	$456.0
New shares from exercised options								
New shares issued from options - millions	2.878	3.341	2.949	3.000	3.000	3.000	3.000	3.000
Average strike price				$30.86	$30.86	$30.86	$30.86	$30.86
Option proceeds	$69.3	$104.7	$122.7	$92.6	$92.6	$92.6	$92.6	$92.6
Dividend assumptions								
Dividends	$184.7	$205.7	$221.2	$267.5	$275.4	$283.7	$292.2	$300.9
Net income	459.1	516.8	567.3	668.8	688.5	709.2	730.4	752.3
Dividend payout ratio	40.2%	39.8%	39.0%	40.0%	40.0%	40.0%	40.0%	40.0%

Calculations

Assumption/Drivers

References (GREEN) from income statement

There are several methods for projecting future dividend payments:

- **Dividend payout ratio**: Assume some dividend payout ratio, based on historical data and trends, and multiply it by projected net income to calculate total projected dividends.

- **Per share basis**: This approach can be used if the company reports how much they expect to pay shareholders on a per-share basis.

  - Calculate total dividends paid by multiplying the dividends to be paid per share by the weighted average number of basic shares for the period. If this is your preferred approach, then wait until we finish the shares outstanding schedule to complete this step.

- **Fixed dollar amount**: This is the simplest method and assumes that a company will pay the same dollar amount (for example, $100 million) every year to shareholders.

As always, to tailor your approach to the particular company and situation(s) you are modeling.

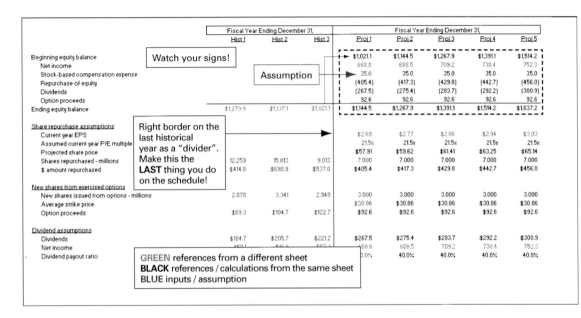

	Fiscal Year Ending December 31,			Fiscal Year Ending December 31,				
	Hist 1	Hist 2	Hist 3	Proj 1	Proj 2	Proj 3	Proj 4	Proj 5
Beginning equity balance				$1,021.1	$1,144.5	$1,267.9	$1,391.1	$1,514.2
Net income				668.8	688.5	709.2	730.4	752.3
Stock-based compensation expense				35.0	35.0	35.0	35.0	35.0
Repurchase of equity				(405.4)	(417.3)	(429.8)	(442.7)	(456.0)
Dividends				(267.5)	(275.4)	(283.7)	(292.2)	(300.9)
Option proceeds				92.6	92.6	92.6	92.6	92.6
Ending equity balance	$1,279.9	$1,137.1	$1,021.1	$1,144.5	$1,267.9	$1,391.1	$1,514.2	$1,637.2
Share repurchase assumptions								
Current year EPS				$2.69	$2.77	$2.86	$2.94	$3.03
Assumed current year P/E multiple				21.5x	21.5x	21.5x	21.5x	21.5x
Projected share price				$57.91	$59.62	$61.41	$63.25	$65.14
Shares repurchased - millions	12.259	15.813	9.013	7.000	7.000	7.000	7.000	7.000
$ amount repurchased	$414.8	$698.9	$537.0	$405.4	$417.3	$429.8	$442.7	$456.0
New shares from exercised options								
New shares issued from options - millions	2.878	3.341	2.343	3.000	3.000	3.000	3.000	3.000
Average strike price				$30.86	$30.86	$30.86	$30.86	$30.86
Option proceeds	$69.3	$104.7	$122.7	$92.6	$92.6	$92.6	$92.6	$92.6
Dividend assumptions								
Dividends	$184.7	$205.7	$221.2	$267.5	$275.4	$283.7	$292.2	$300.9
Net income				668.8	688.5	709.2	730.4	752.3
Dividend payout ratio				40.0%	40.0%	40.0%	40.0%	40.0%

Callouts within figure:
- Watch your signs!
- Assumption
- Right border on the last historical year as a "divider". Make this the **LAST** thing you do on the schedule!
- GREEN references from a different sheet
  BLACK references / calculations from the same sheet
  BLUE inputs / assumption

Corkscrew the shareholders' equity balance. Recall that a corkscrew involves making the beginning balance for one period equal to the ending balance from the previous year.

– A corkscrew or turn is a method of forecasting a projected balance. Let's walk through a corkscrew.

Reference projected net income from the income statement. Be careful with your signs here: Net income should be positive because it increases shareholders' equity.

Make an assumption to project share-based compensation.

– Look for historical detail in the company's financial footnotes or on the cash flow statement (toward the top under operating activities) to help guide your assumption for projected periods.

Reference Repurchase of equity (in dollars). Be careful with your signs here: This number should be negative because, when a company repurchases shares, the shares are removed from circulation, thereby reducing shareholders' equity.

Reference Dividends (in dollars). Since dividends reduce retained earnings and thereby shareholders' equity, this number should be negative.

Reference Option proceeds. Since option proceeds represent a cash inflow from options being exercised, this number should be positive.

Calculate the ending equity balance by summing the line items above.

 Please view the Online Companion for related supplementary media.

STEP 51

Link shareholders' equity projections to the balance sheet

NOTES

	Fiscal Year Ending December 31,			Fiscal Year Ending December 31,				
	Hist 1	Hist 2	Hist 3	Proj 1	Proj 2	Proj 3	Proj 4	Proj 5
Cash	$114.8	$54.8	$67.2					
Accounts receivable, net	407.6	408.9	559.3	573.2	590.4	608.1	626.3	645.1
Inventories	492.9	557.2	610.3	626.2	645.0	664.3	684.2	704.8
Other current assets	116.3	176.7	172.2	179.3	184.7	190.2	195.9	201.8
Total current assets	1,131.6	1,197.7	1,408.9					
PP&E, net	1,661.9	1,682.7	1,659.1	1,664.1	1,667.0	1,668.9	1,669.9	1,669.9
Definite life intangibles	46.2	61.0	65.1	63.1	61.6	60.6	60.1	60.1
Indefinite life intangibles	31.6	100.3	111.9	111.9	111.9	111.9	111.9	111.9
Goodwill	389.0	463.9	487.3	487.3	487.3	487.3	487.3	487.3
Other long-term assets	322.3	307.1	562.8	562.8	0.0	562.8	0.0	562.8
Total assets	**$3,582.5**	**$3,812.8**	**$4,295.2**					
Accounts payable	$132.2	$148.7	$167.8	$171.1	$176.3	$181.5	$187.0	$192.6
Accrued liabilities	416.2	469.2	507.8	522.4	538.1	554.2	570.9	588.0
Other current liabilities	24.9	42.3	23.5	22.7	23.4	24.1	24.8	25.6
Total current liabilities	573.3	660.2	699.1					
Revolver	12.0	343.3	81.4					
Long-term debt	969.0	969.6	1,680.5					
Deferred income taxes	377.6	319.2	400.3	400.3	400.3	400.3	400.3	400.3
Other long-term liabilities	370.8	383.4	412.9	412.9	412.9	412.9	412.9	412.9
Total liabilities	2,302.7	2,675.7	3,274.2					
Total equity	1,279.9	1,137.1	1,021.1	1,144.5	1,267.9	1,391.1	1,514.2	1,637.2
Total liabilities and equity	**$3,582.5**	**$3,812.8**	**$4,295.2**					
Parity check (A=L+E)	0.000	0.000	0.000					

References

Link projected ending equity balance to the balance sheet.

Remember that the balance sheet represents values at one particular point in time: the last day of the period (for example, Hist 3).

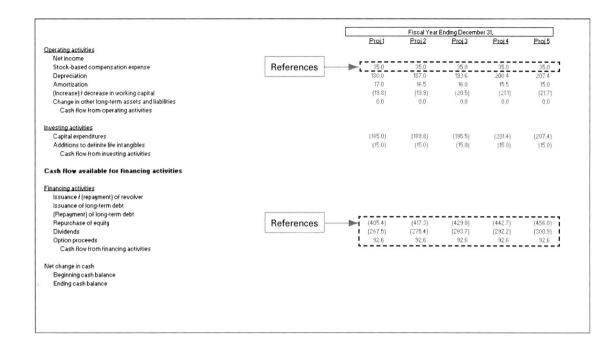

NOTES

Link projected stock-based compensation expense to the cash flow statement (toward the top of the page).

– Be careful with your signs—stock-based compensation expense should be positive here. It is being added back to net income as a non-cash expense.

Link projected repurchase of equity and dividends to the financing activities section of the cash flow statement.

– Be careful with your signs—these items should be negative because they represent cash outflows.

Link projected option proceeds to the financing activities section of the cash flow statement.

– Careful with your signs—option proceeds should be positive here because they represent cash inflows from option holders who exercise their options.

Flow-of-funds

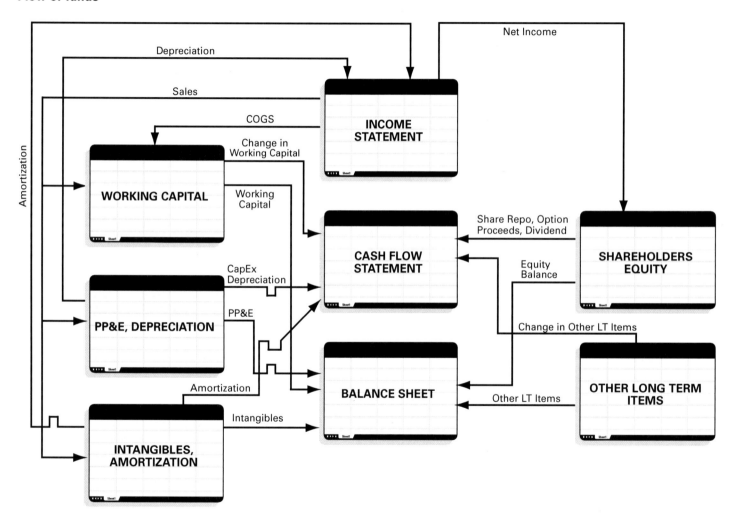

Stress Testing

As with any completed schedule, it is important to understand how the drivers on the shareholders' equity schedule work, and how to "turn off" and "turn on" certain features.

Take, for example, the share repurchase section of our shareholders' equity schedule. This section is primarily controlled by two drivers: the P/E multiple, which determines the price at which shares are repurchased, and the number of shares repurchased. We can stress-test this section by "turning off" share repurchases. How?

Since there are two drivers, we may be equally inclined to "zero out" either of them. That is, we may be thinking, erroneously, that entering a value of zero for either the P/E multiple or the number of shares repurchased will accomplish the same end: namely, to nullify the effect of share repurchases on our model.

However, recognize the subtle distinction between the two methods. If, for example, we were to zero out the P/E multiple while making no change to the number of shares repurchased, then the company would effectively spend no money on share repurchases, which would seem to suit our purpose. However, maintaining the number of shares repurchased is problematic because, in subsequent steps, we will rely on this driver to calculate number of shares on our shares outstanding schedule, which will eventually be linked to the income statement.

We therefore recommend an alternative method: zero out the number of shares repurchased and leave the P/E assumption intact. This allows us to safely observe the impact of share repurchases on our model while avoiding potential errors in subsequent steps.

As with every stress test, be sure to change the assumption cells back to their original state after the test is completed and you are satisfied that the formulas in your model are working properly.

 Please view the Online Companion for related supplementary media.

4.8 SHARES OUTSTANDING SCHEDULE

Recall that in previous steps, we flatlined the shares outstanding on the income statement in order to "temporarily" calculate earnings per share. Our purpose for creating these "placeholder" values was to forecast the number of shares repurchased on the shareholders' equity schedule. Now, we will use the shares outstanding schedule to project shares outstanding and replace the flatline logic and placeholder values on the income statement.

Note that companies report several types of shares on their financial statements:

Actual shares – This is the share count as of a certain date. For example, on March 31, 20X9, Company ABC had 40,383,328 shares outstanding.

Weighted average shares – This is a "time-weighted" share count that reflects shares issued or repurchased over a given period. For example, if Company ABC issues 5,000,000 million shares in the middle of their fiscal year, the weighted average share count would increase by 2,500,000 (or 5,000,000 x the ½ year that the share issuance was in effect).

In addition to timing differences, there are also differences between **basic shares outstanding** and **diluted shares outstanding**. Diluted shares reflect the effects of options and dilutive securities (i.e., convertible debt) on a company's shares outstanding.

Bearing these differences in mind, we'll approach this schedule by first referencing the relevant projections from the shareholders' equity schedule, including shares repurchased and new shares from exercised options. We will then project actual basic shares and calculate average

basic and diluted shares outstanding. Finally, we will link projected shares to the income statement, replacing the temporary flatline logic built in previous steps.

Shares Outstanding Table for TTS Sample Company

Dollars in millions, except per share data

	Fiscal Year Ending December 31,			Fiscal Year Ending December 31,				
	Hist 1	Hist 2	Hist 3	Proj 1	Proj 2	Proj 3	Proj 4	Proj 5
Beginning balance - basic (actual)								
Shares issued from options	*Historicals not needed*							
Shares repurchased								
Ending balance - basic (actual)	259.059	246.588	240.524					
Average basic shares	262.612	253.881	244.568					
Effects of dilutive securities	1.920	3.053	3.724					
Average diluted shares	264.532	256.934	248.292					

BLUE inputs

BLACK calculations

Note: This table is shown as a separate schedule, but it is
commonly placed on the equity schedule.

NOTES

Set up the line items for the shares outstanding schedule.

Input historical data for basic (actual) shares, average basic shares, and effects of dilutive securities.

– Data can be found in the company filings or company-provided financial reports.

– The balance for basic (actual) shares outstanding can be found in the statement of shareholders' equity balance sheet (or sometimes in the footnotes).

– Average basic shares and the effects of dilutive securities can usually be found in the earnings per share footnote, or at the bottom of the income statement.

Calculate average diluted shares by summing average basic shares and the effects of dilutive securities.

Note that although we've elected to create a separate supporting schedule to project shares outstanding, this information could also be consolidated onto the shareholders' equity schedule.

STEP 54

Project basic shares

NOTES

	Fiscal Year Ending December 31,			Fiscal Year Ending December 31,				
	Hist 1	Hist 2	Hist 3	Proj 1	Proj 2	Proj 3	Proj 4	Proj 5
Beginning balance - basic (actual)				240.524	236.524	232.524	228.524	224.524
Shares issued from options				3.000	3.000	3.000	3.000	3.000
Shares repurchased				(7.000)	(7.000)	(7.000)	(7.000)	(7.000)
Ending balance - basic (actual)	259.059	246.588	240.524	236.524	232.524	228.524	224.524	220.524
Average basic shares	262.612	253.881	244.568					
Effects of dilutive securities	1.920	3.053	3.724					
Average diluted shares	264.532	256.934	248.292					

References

Calculations

GREEN references from a different sheet
BLACK references or calculations from the same sheet
BLUE inputs or assumptions

Corkscrew the ending balance of basic (actual) shares by making the beginning balance for one period equal to the ending balance from the previous year.

Reference shares issued from options and shares repurchased from the shareholders' equity schedule.

– Be careful with your signs: shares issued from options should be positive, and shares repurchased should be negative.

Calculate projected ending balances of basic (actual) shares by summing the line items above.

	Fiscal Year Ending December 31,			Fiscal Year Ending December 31,				
	Hist 1	Hist 2	Hist 3	Proj 1	Proj 2	Proj 3	Proj 4	Proj 5
Beginning balance - basic (actual)				240.524	236.524	232.524	228.524	224.524
Shares issued from options				3.000	3.000	3.000	3.000	3.000
Shares repurchased				(7.000)	(7.000)	(7.000)	(7.000)	(7.000)
Ending balance - basic (actual)	259.059	248.588	240.524	236.524	232.524	228.524	224.524	220.524
Average basic shares	262.612	253.881	244.568	238.524	234.524	230.524	226.524	222.524
Effects of dilutive securities	1.920	3.053	3.724					
Average diluted shares	264.532	256.934	248.292					

Calculations

NOTES

Calculate average basic shares by averaging the beginning basic shares balance and the ending basic shares balance.

We take an average here because it is difficult to predict the precise timing of a company's share issuances and repurchases. Our approach assumes that the company is issuing and repurchasing the shares evenly throughout the year.

NOTES

	Fiscal Year Ending December 31,			Fiscal Year Ending December 31,				
	Hist 1	Hist 2	Hist 3	Proj 1	Proj 2	Proj 3	Proj 4	Proj 5
Beginning balance - basic (actual)				240.524	236.524	232.524	228.524	224.524
Shares issued from options				3.000	3.000	3.000	3.000	3.000
Shares repurchased				(7.000)	(7.000)	(7.000)	(7.000)	(7.000)
Ending balance - basic (actual)	259.059	246.588	240.524	236.524	232.524	228.524	224.524	220.524
Average basic shares	262.612	253.881	244.568	238.524	234.524	230.524	226.524	222.524
Effects of dilutive securities	1.920	3.053	3.724	3.724	3.724	3.724	3.724	3.724
Average diluted shares	264.532	256.934	248.292	242.248	238.248	234.248	230.248	226.248

Right border on the last historical year as a "divider". Make this the **LAST** thing you do on the schedule!

Assumption

Calculations

Questions
– What is the common use of weighted average BASIC shares?
– What is the common use of weighted average DILUTED shares?

Answers
– Weighted average BASIC shares is used to calculate basic EPS and dividends per share.
– Weighted average DILUTED shares is used to calculate diluted EPS.

Make a reasonable assumption for the effects of dilutive securities based on historical periods.

– Unless you have access to better information, consider using the value from the last historical period and flatlining it across the projected periods.

Calculate average diluted shares by summing average basic shares and effects of dilutive securities.

	Fiscal Year Ending December 31,			Fiscal Year Ending December 31,					5 Year CAGR
	Hist 1	Hist 2	Hist 3	Proj 1	Proj 2	Proj 3	Proj 4	Proj 5	
Sales	$4,172.6								3.0%
Cost of goods sold, excluding depreciation (1)	2,383.7								
Gross profit	1,788.9								3.1%
SG&A expenses, excluding amortization	819.5								
Other operating (income) / expenses	0.0								
EBITDA	969.4								3.6%
Depreciation (1)	158.9								
Amortization	21.6								
EBIT (2)	788.8								3.8%
Interest expense	65.3	67.9	89.5						
Interest (income)	(1.7)	(1.4)	(1.5)						
Other non-operating (income) / expense	0.0	0.0	0.0	0.0	0.0	0.0	0.0	0.0	
Pretax income	725.3	815.2	891.9	1,048.3	1,079.1	1,111.5	1,144.9	1,179.1	5.7%
Income taxes (3)			324.7	379.5	390.6	402.4	414.4	426.8	
Net income (4)			$567.3	$668.8	$688.5	$709.2	$730.4	$752.3	5.8%
Diluted weighted average shares in millions			248.292	242.248	238.248	234.248	230.248	226.248	(1.8%)
Earnings per share	$1.74	$2.01	$2.28	$2.76	$2.89	$3.03	$3.17	$3.33	7.8%
Ratios & assumptions									
Sales growth rate		6.2%	9.2%	3.0%		3.0%	3.0%	3.0%	
Gross margin	42.9%	43.3%	42.8%	43.0%	43.0%	43.0%	43.0%	43.0%	
SG&A expenses (as a % of sales)	19.6%	19.2%	18.5%	18.0%	18.0%	18.0%	18.0%	18.0%	
Other operating (income) / expenses ($ amount)	$0.0	$0.0	$0.0	$0.0	$0.0	$0.0	$0.0	$0.0	
Other non-operating (income) / expense ($ amount)	0.0	0.0	0.0	0.0	0.0	0.0	0.0	0.0	
Effective tax rate	36.7%	36.6%	36.4%	36.2%	36.2%	36.2%	36.2%	36.2%	

Question:
– What impact will linking in these numbers have on your model?

Answer:
– Linking in the shares will change your EPS number and all of the items dependent on EPS (for example, such as share repurchase).

Change the color to GREEN, if you made these RED in a previous step.

References

Link projected average diluted shares to the income statement.

– We made these cells red earlier to remind us that they were placeholders whose flatline logic needed to be replaced. Now that these cells are references to another sheet, you should change them from red to green.

Iterative Equity Schedule

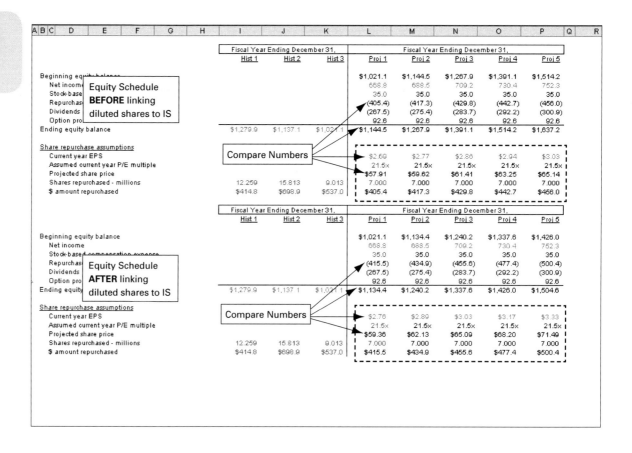

Stress Testing: Using Iterativity to Test a Model

At this stage in our modeling process, we've created a series of relationships in Excel that makes our model **iterative**. A model is said to be iterative when changes in certain items set off chain reactions that cause several other items to change.

For example, let's say you make an assumption that alters the number of shares repurchased on the shareholders' equity schedule. This would cause the number of diluted shares to change on the shares outstanding schedule. Since diluted shares are now linked to the income statement, there would be an effect on earnings per share. Recall that earnings per share were previously linked from the income statement to the shareholders' equity schedule in order to determine the share price at which shares would be repurchased. A change in earnings per share would therefore impact the dollar amount of shares repurchased.

This sequence illustrates the iterative nature of the model you've created so far. To test this phenomenon, change an assumption related to shares outstanding on any of your core statements or supporting schedules. Observe the ripple effect flowing through the other areas of your model. So far, we've used stress tests to verify that the logic on a *single* row or worksheet was working properly. This test goes further, revealing the dynamic, interdependent relationships between your model's core statements and various supporting schedules. Keep this important concept in mind as we complete our final steps together.

Please view the Online Companion for related supplementary media.

4.9 PREPARING FOR DEBT AND INTEREST

Our final supporting schedule accounts for the effect of debt financing on our company's core statements. Before we can consider the effects of debt, however, we must first understand our company's need for and ability to finance debt capital based on its residual cash flows. By residual cash flows we mean the company's cash flows from operations that are available for financing (that is, after capital investments have been made). Before building the debt and interest schedule, therefore, we must first build some logic on the cash flow statement. Exhibit 5.1 illustrates the logical progression of a typical cash flow statement:

To complete the cash flow statement logic, we first calculate

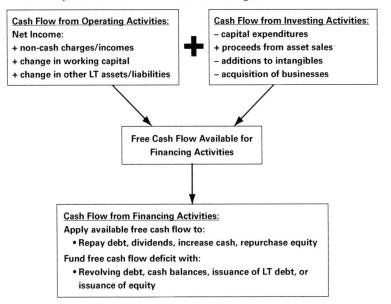

cash flow from operating and investing activities. We then calculate cash flow available for financing activities, which will ultimately be linked to the debt and interest schedule. The main purpose of this section of the model is to determine whether the company has a surplus of cash flow enabling it to pay down its debt balance, or a shortfall of cash flow requiring it to increase its debt balance.

Before we begin, remember that the cash flow statement calculates the change in cash flow during a given period:

To calculate the ending cash balance in a period, we add

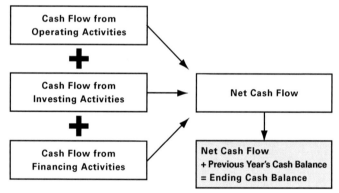

the net change in cash flow to that period's beginning cash balance. We then link the ending cash balance back to the balance sheet.

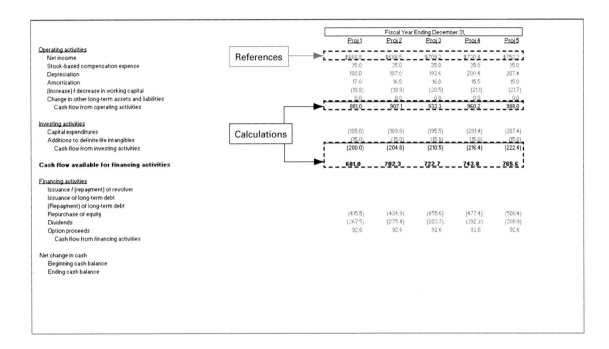

| | Fiscal Year Ending December 31, | | | | |
	Proj 1	Proj 2	Proj 3	Proj 4	Proj 5
Operating activities					
Net income	$668.8	$688.5	$709.2	$730.4	$752.3
Stock-based compensation expense	35.0	35.0	35.0	35.0	35.0
Depreciation	180.0	187.0	193.6	200.4	207.4
Amortization	17.0	16.5	16.0	15.5	15.0
(Increase) / decrease in working capital	(19.3)	(19.9)	(20.5)	(21.1)	(21.7)
Change in other long-term assets and liabilities	0.0	0.0	0.0	0.0	0.0
Cash flow from operating activities	881.0	907.1	933.3	960.2	988.0
Investing activities					
Capital expenditures	(185.0)	(189.8)	(195.5)	(201.4)	(207.4)
Additions to definite life intangibles	(15.0)	(15.0)	(15.0)	(15.0)	(15.0)
Cash flow from investing activities	(200.0)	(204.8)	(210.5)	(216.4)	(222.4)
Cash flow available for financing activities	681.0	702.3	722.7	743.8	765.6
Financing activities					
Issuance / (repayment) of revolver					
Issuance of long-term debt					
(Repayment) of long-term debt					
Repurchase of equity	(415.5)	(434.9)	(455.6)	(477.4)	(500.4)
Dividends	(267.5)	(275.4)	(283.7)	(292.2)	(300.9)
Option proceeds	92.6	92.6	92.6	92.6	92.6
Cash flow from financing activities					
Net change in cash					
Beginning cash balance					
Ending cash balance					

References

Calculations

NOTES

Link *net income* from the income statement to the cash flow statement (the first line).

Calculate (1) cash flow from operating activities, (2) cash flow from investing activities, and (3) cash flow available for financing activities.

 Please view the Online Companion for related supplementary media.

STEP 59

Calculate Cash Flow from Financing Activities and Net Change in Cash

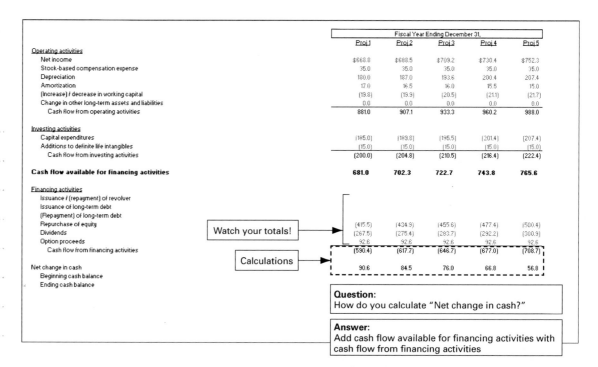

	Fiscal Year Ending December 31,				
	Proj 1	Proj 2	Proj 3	Proj 4	Proj 5
Operating activities					
Net income	$688.8	$688.5	$709.2	$730.4	$752.3
Stock-based compensation expense	35.0	35.0	35.0	35.0	35.0
Depreciation	180.0	187.0	193.6	200.4	207.4
Amortization	17.0	16.5	16.0	15.5	15.0
(Increase) / decrease in working capital	(19.8)	(19.3)	(20.5)	(21.1)	(21.7)
Change in other long-term assets and liabilities	0.0	0.0	0.0	0.0	0.0
Cash flow from operating activities	881.0	907.1	933.3	960.2	988.0
Investing activities					
Capital expenditures	(185.0)	(189.8)	(195.5)	(201.4)	(207.4)
Additions to definite life intangibles	(15.0)	(15.0)	(15.0)	(15.0)	(15.0)
Cash flow from investing activities	(200.0)	(204.8)	(210.5)	(216.4)	(222.4)
Cash flow available for financing activities	**681.0**	**702.3**	**722.7**	**743.8**	**765.6**
Financing activities					
Issuance / (repayment) of revolver					
Issuance of long-term debt					
(Repayment) of long-term debt					
Repurchase of equity	(415.5)	(434.9)	(455.6)	(477.4)	(500.4)
Dividends	(267.5)	(275.4)	(283.7)	(292.2)	(300.9)
Option proceeds	92.6	92.6	92.6	92.6	92.6
Cash flow from financing activities	(590.4)	(617.7)	(646.7)	(677.0)	(708.7)
Net change in cash	90.6	84.5	76.0	66.8	56.8
Beginning cash balance					
Ending cash balance					

Watch your totals! →

Calculations →

Question:
How do you calculate "Net change in cash?"

Answer:
Add cash flow available for financing activities with cash flow from financing activities

---

Calculate cash flow from financing activities by summing all the line items related to financing activities.

– Be careful when using the auto-sum feature, because this will not automatically capture the blank rows in this section (that is, the three rows above repurchase of equity). You need to adjust the range manually to include all the rows that relate to financing activities (that is, all the rows from issuance/(repayment) of revolver to option proceeds).

Calculate net change in cash by adding together cash flow from financing activities and cash flow available for financing activities.

 Please view the Online Companion for related supplementary media.

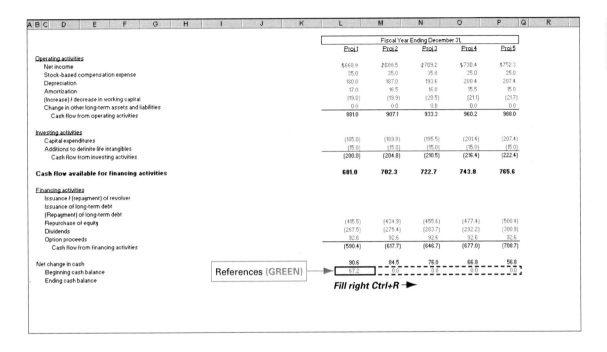

	Fiscal Year Ending December 31,				
	Proj 1	Proj 2	Proj 3	Proj 4	Proj 5
Operating activities					
Net income	$668.8	$688.5	$709.2	$730.4	$752.3
Stock-based compensation expense	35.0	35.0	35.0	35.0	35.0
Depreciation	180.0	187.0	193.6	200.4	207.4
Amortization	17.0	16.5	16.0	15.5	15.0
(Increase) / decrease in working capital	(19.8)	(19.9)	(20.5)	(21.1)	(21.7)
Change in other long-term assets and liabilities	0.0	0.0	0.0	0.0	0.0
Cash flow from operating activities	881.0	907.1	933.3	960.2	988.0
Investing activities					
Capital expenditures	(185.0)	(189.8)	(195.5)	(201.4)	(207.4)
Additions to definite life intangibles	(15.0)	(15.0)	(15.0)	(15.0)	(15.0)
Cash flow from investing activities	(200.0)	(204.8)	(210.5)	(216.4)	(222.4)
Cash flow available for financing activities	**681.0**	**702.3**	**722.7**	**743.8**	**765.6**
Financing activities					
Issuance / (repayment) of revolver					
Issuance of long-term debt					
(Repayment) of long-term debt					
Repurchase of equity	(415.5)	(434.9)	(455.6)	(477.4)	(500.4)
Dividends	(267.5)	(275.4)	(283.7)	(292.2)	(300.9)
Option proceeds	92.6	92.6	92.6	92.6	92.6
Cash flow from financing activities	(590.4)	(617.7)	(646.7)	(677.0)	(708.7)
Net change in cash	90.6	84.5	76.0	66.8	56.8
Beginning cash balance	67.2	0.0	0.0	0.0	0.0
Ending cash balance					

References (GREEN)

Fill right Ctrl+R ➤

NOTES

Reference beginning cash balance from the balance sheet.

Watch your column references! Be sure to make the beginning cash balance for one period equal to the ending cash balance from the prior period (for example, the beginning cash balance on Proj 1 should be equal to the ending cash balance on Hist 3).

Trust The Steps!!!

	Hist 1	Hist 2	Hist 3	Proj 1	Proj 2	Proj 3	Proj 4
	Fiscal Year Ending December 31,			Fiscal Year Ending December 31,			
Cash	$114.8	$54.8	$67.2				
Accounts receivable, net	407.6	408.9	559.3	573.2	590.4	608.1	626.3
Inventories	492.9	557.2	610.3	626.2	645.0	664.3	684.2
Other current assets	116.3	176.7	172.2	179.3	184.7	190.2	195.9
Total current assets	1,131.6	1,197.7	1,408.9				
PP&E, net	1,661.9	1,682.7				18.9	1,669.9
Definite life intangibles	46.2	61.0				0.6	60.1
Indefinite life intangibles	31.6	100.3				1.9	111.9
Goodwill	389.0	463.9				7.3	487.3
Other long-term assets	322.3	307.1				2.8	0.0
Total assets	**$3,582.5**	**$3,812.8**	$				
Accounts payable	$132.2	$148.7	$167.8	$171.1	$176.3	$181.6	$187.0
Accrued liabilities	416.2	469.2	507.8	522.4	538.1	554.2	570.9
Other current liabilities	24.9	42.3	23.5	22.7	23.4	24.1	24.8
Total current liabilities	573.3	660.2	699.1				
Revolver	12.0	343.3	81.4				
Long-term debt	969.0	969.6	1,680.5				
Deferred income taxes	377.6	319.2	400.3	400.3	400.3	400.3	400.3
Other long-term liabilities	370.8	383.4	412.9	412.9	412.9	412.9	412.9
Total liabilities	2,302.7	2,675.7	3,274.2				
Total equity	1,279.9	1,137.1	1,021.1	1,134.4	1,240.2	1,337.6	1,426.0
Total liabilities and equity	**$3,582.5**	**$3,812.8**	**$4,295.2**				
Parity check (A = L + E)	*0.000*	*0.000*	*0.000*				

Trust The Steps
- Note: Projected cash has yet to be linked
- Excel reads blank cells as zeros
- Projected cash will be linked on the next step

NOTES

STEP 61
. . . .
Calculate ending cash balance
on the cash flow statement

	Fiscal Year Ending December 31,				
	Proj 1	Proj 2	Proj 3	Proj 4	Proj 5
Operating activities					
Net income	$868.8	$888.5	$709.2	$730.4	$752.3
Stock-based compensation expense	35.0	35.0	35.0	35.0	35.0
Depreciation	180.0	187.0	193.6	200.4	207.4
Amortization	17.0	16.5	16.0	15.5	15.0
(Increase) / decrease in working capital	(13.8)	(13.9)	(20.5)	(21.1)	(21.7)
Change in other long-term assets and liabilities	0.0	0.0	0.0	0.0	0.0
Cash flow from operating activities	881.0	907.1	933.3	960.2	988.0
Investing activities					
Capital expenditures	(185.0)	(189.8)	(195.5)	(201.4)	(207.4)
Additions to definite life intangibles	(15.0)	(15.0)	(15.0)	(15.0)	(15.0)
Cash flow from investing activities	(200.0)	(204.8)	(210.5)	(216.4)	(222.4)
Cash flow available for financing activities	**681.0**	**702.3**	**722.7**	**743.8**	**765.6**
Financing activities					
Issuance / (repayment) of revolver					
Issuance of long-term debt					
(Repayment) of long-term debt					
Repurchase of equity	(415.5)	(434.9)	(455.6)	(477.4)	(500.4)
Dividends	(267.5)	(275.4)	(283.7)	(292.2)	(300.9)
Option proceeds	92.6	92.6	92.6	92.6	92.6
Cash flow from financing activities	(590.4)	(617.7)	(646.7)	(677.0)	(708.7)
Net change in cash	90.6	84.5	76.0	66.8	56.8
Beginning cash balance	67.2	0.0	0.0	0.0	0.0
Ending cash balance → Calculations	$157.8	$84.5	$76.0	$66.8	$56.8

Calculate the ending cash balance on the cash flow statement by adding together the beginning cash balance and the net change in cash.
. . . .

– Be careful! This step needs to be performed on the cash flow statement first; the projected ending cash balances will be linked to the balance sheet in the next step.

STEP 62

Link the ending cash balance from the cash flow statement to the balance sheet

NOTES

	Fiscal Year Ending December 31,			Fiscal Year Ending December 31,				
	Hist 1	Hist 2	Hist 3	Proj 1	Proj 2	Proj 3	Proj 4	Proj 5
Cash	$114.8	$54.8	$67.2	$157.8	$242.3	$318.4	$385.2	$442.0
Accounts receivable, net	407.6	408.9	559.3	573.2	590.4	608.1	626.3	645.1
Inventories	492.9	557.2	610.3	626.2	645.0	664.3	684.2	704.8
Other current assets	116.3	176.7	172.2	179.3	184.7	190.2	195.9	201.8
Total current assets	1,131.6	1,197.7	1,408.9					
PP&E, net	1,661.9	1,682.7	1,659.1		1,668.9	1,668.9	1,668.9	1,668.9
Definite life intangibles	46.2	61.0	65.1	63.1	61.6	60.6	60.1	60.1
Indefinite life intangibles	31.6	100.3	111.9	111.9	111.9	111.9	111.9	111.9
Goodwill	389.0	463.9	487.3	487.3	487.3	487.3	487.3	487.3
Other long-term assets	322.3	307.1	562.8	562.8	0.0	562.8	0.0	562.8
Total assets	**$3,582.5**	**$3,812.8**	**$4,295.2**					
Accounts payable	$132.2	$148.7	$167.8	$171.1	$176.3	$181.6	$187.0	$192.6
Accrued liabilities	416.2	463.2	507.8	522.4	538.1	554.2	570.9	588.0
Other current liabilities	24.9	42.3	23.5	22.7	23.4	24.1	24.8	25.6
Total current liabilities	573.3	660.2	699.1					
Revolver	12.0	343.3	81.4					
Long-term debt	969.0	963.6	1,680.5					
Deferred income taxes	377.6	319.2	400.3	400.3	400.3	400.3	400.3	400.3
Other long-term liabilities	370.8	383.4	412.9	412.9	412.9	412.9	412.9	412.9
Total liabilities	2,302.7	2,675.7	3,274.2					
Total equity	1,279.9	1,137.1	1,021.1	1,134.4	1,240.2	1,337.6	1,426.0	1,504.6
Total liabilities and equity	**$3,582.5**	**$3,812.8**	**$4,295.2**					
Parity check (A=L+E)	*0.000*	*0.000*	*0.000*					

Trust the Steps!

References

Link the ending cash balance calculated in Step 61 to the projected cash balance on the balance sheet (at the top of the balance sheet).

– Again, be careful with your column references here – make sure you are linking the correct years. Also, be careful to link the ending cash balance to the balance sheet, not the beginning cash balance.

Observe that you have now created an iterative balance sheet and cash flow statement.

– Your cash balance is determined by your cash flow; your cash flow is affected by how much net income you have; your net income is affected by your interest income; and your interest income is calculated based on your cash balance. This series of relationships has advanced the iterative nature of your model.

 Please view the Online Companion for related supplementary media.

Iterative Cash Flow and Balance Sheet

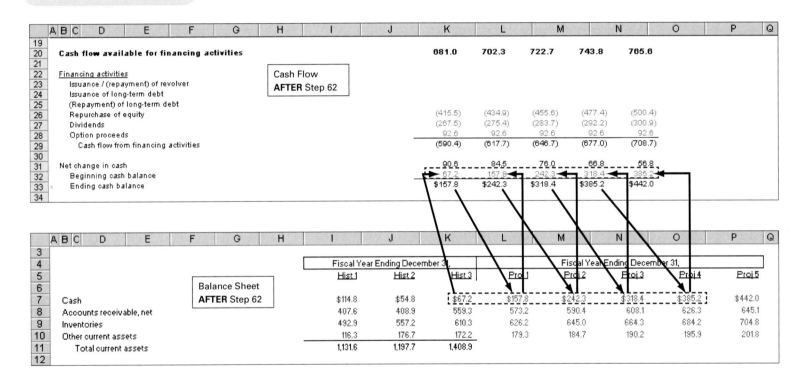

				K	L	M	N	O		
19										
20	**Cash flow available for financing activities**			681.0	702.3	722.7	743.8	765.6		
21										
22	Financing activities									
23	Issuance / (repayment) of revolver									
24	Issuance of long-term debt									
25	(Repayment) of long-term debt									
26	Repurchase of equity			(415.5)	(434.9)	(455.6)	(477.4)	(500.4)		
27	Dividends			(267.5)	(275.4)	(283.7)	(292.2)	(300.9)		
28	Option proceeds			92.6	92.6	92.6	92.6	92.6		
29	Cash flow from financing activities			(590.4)	(617.7)	(646.7)	(677.0)	(708.7)		
30										
31	Net change in cash			90.6	84.5	76.0	66.8	56.8		
32	Beginning cash balance			67.2	157.8	242.3	318.4	385.2		
33	Ending cash balance			$157.8	$242.3	$318.4	$385.2	$442.0		
34										

Cash Flow **AFTER** Step 62

						I	J	K	L	M	N	O	P
3													
4						Fiscal Year Ending December 31,			Fiscal Year Ending December 31,				
5						Hist 1	Hist 2	Hist 3	Proj 1	Proj 2	Proj 3	Proj 4	Proj 5
6													
7	Cash					$114.8	$54.8	$67.2	$157.8	$242.3	$318.4	$385.2	$442.0
8	Accounts receivable, net					407.6	408.9	559.3	573.2	590.4	608.1	626.3	645.1
9	Inventories					492.9	557.2	610.3	626.2	645.0	664.3	684.2	704.8
10	Other current assets					116.3	176.7	172.2	179.3	184.7	190.2	195.9	201.8
11	Total current assets					1,131.6	1,197.7	1,408.9					
12													

Balance Sheet **AFTER** Step 62

NOTES

Flow-of-funds

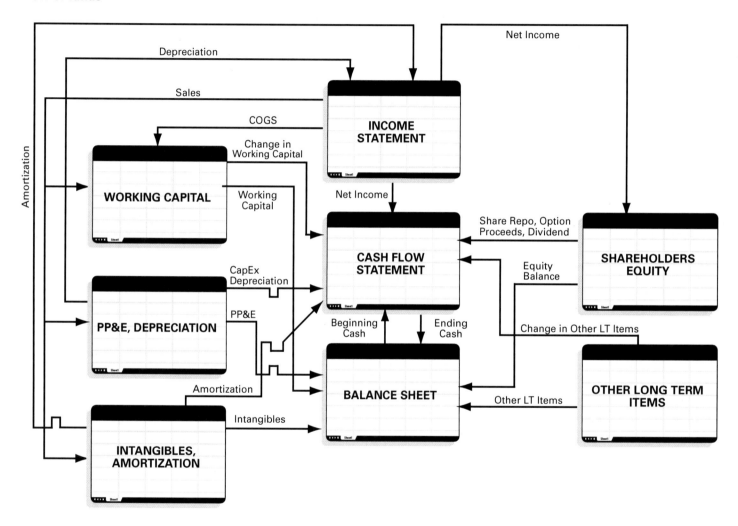

Note that, for the first time, the core statements are now directly linked to each other. The income statement links to the cash flow statement via the *net income* line. The cash flow statement links to the balance sheet via the *ending cash balance* line.

However, at this stage, there is no direct link from the balance sheet and cash flow statement back to the income statement. That is, the relationship is still one-way, or unidirectional. The debt and interest schedule will provide an indirect link back to the income statement.

Stress Testing

Let's check the logic of our formulas and references. Refer back to the calculation of cash flow from financing activities on the cash flow statement. Does the sum function capture the revolver and long-term debt items? It is easy to miss these items since they are blank (for now). It is critical to build the formula correctly since these items will eventually be referenced from the debt and interest schedule.

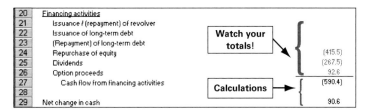

Go back to the step where you linked *beginning balance of cash* from the balance sheet to the cash flow statement. Did you reference the correct column? It is easy to reference the wrong year's balance because you are constructing a formula that references a different column on a separate sheet. This value should come from <u>last year's cash balance</u> on the balance sheet.

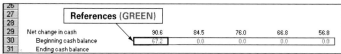

Please view the Online Companion for related supplementary media.

4.10 DEBT AND INTEREST SCHEDULE

We are almost done building our model. At this stage, we are ready to account for the effects of debt financing on the company's core statements. We will model the accounts of two kinds of debt: long-term debt and short-term debt, which we call the **revolving credit facility**.

A revolving credit facility (sometimes called a **revolver** or **line of credit**) acts essentially like a company's credit card. It can be "drawn down" (or borrowed against) when a company needs to cover short-term expenses (for example, working capital needs). If a company has an outstanding balance on its revolver, it can use residual cash flows (that is, operating cash flows after capital investments) to pay down the balance.

In our model, we use the revolving credit facility as a "cash sweep." That is, after evaluating a company's operating, investing, mandatory financing, and shareholder equity activities, we use the revolver to address any remaining cash needs. If the company has a cash flow surplus, then we "sweep" excess cash to the revolver (that is, use cash to pay down the revolver balance).

The long-term debt balance captures the collective claims of all other debt holders. To model this balance, we first reference historical balances from our balance sheet, then input mandatory long-term debt repayments scheduled for future periods. We will reference the company's 10-K or annual report to source this information.

Forecasting debt balances allows us to directly calculate future interest expense from debt. We will also model the interest income we expect the company to earn from cash balances. Again, we will reference company filings to determine relevant interest rates in our calculations.

To complete the model, we will link the relevant items from our debt and interest schedule back to our core statements. To do this, we will first link projected debt *issuance* and *repayment* to the cash flow statement. Next, we will link projected debt balances to the balance sheet. Finally, we will link projected *interest expense* and *interest income* to the income statement.

Debt and Interest Schedule for TTS Sample Company

Dollars in millions, except per share data

	Fiscal Year Ending December 31,			Fiscal Year Ending December 31,				
	Hist 1	Hist 2	Hist 3	Proj 1	Proj 2	Proj 3	Proj 4	Proj 5
Cash flow available for financing activities				$681.0	$702.3	$722.7	$743.8	$765.6
Repurchase of equity				(415.5)	(434.9)	(455.6)	(477.4)	(500.4)
Dividends				(267.5)	(275.4)	(283.7)	(292.2)	(300.9)
Option proceeds				92.6	92.6	92.6	92.6	92.6
Plus: beginning cash balance								
Less: minimum cash balance								
Cash available for debt repayment								
Long-term debt issuance								
Long-term debt (repayment)								
Excess cash available for revolver								
Revolver								
Beginning balance								
Issuance / (repayment) of revolver								
Ending balance								
Long-term debt								
Beginning balance								
Issuance								
(Repayment)								
Ending balance								

References →

Revolver	Average balances							
	Interest rate							
	Interest expense							
Long-term debt	Average balances							
	Interest rate							
	Interest expense							
	Total interest expense							
Cash	Average balances							
	Interest rate							
	Interest (income)							

Create the line items as follows:

- Reference cash flow available for financing activities from the cash flow statement (located right below the investing activities section).

- Reference the second half of the financing activities section, which are the lines we've completed already (repurchase of equity, dividends, and option proceeds).

  - Think of these items as the equity sources and uses of cash. We include them here because if the company does not have enough cash to cover these expenses (for example, to pay dividends), then we assume it will use debt financing (that is , borrow more) to do so.

NOTES

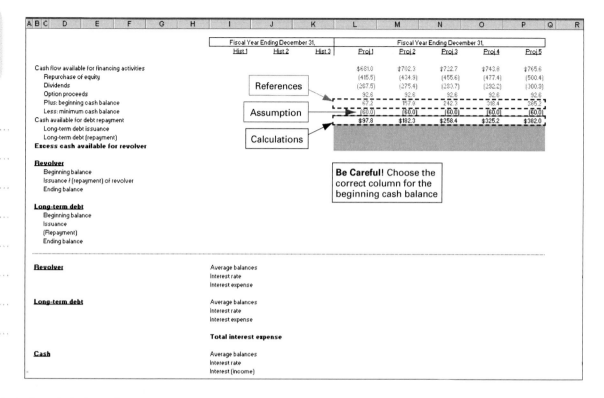

		Fiscal Year Ending December 31,			Fiscal Year Ending December 31,				
		Hist 1	Hist 2	Hist 3	Proj 1	Proj 2	Proj 3	Proj 4	Proj 5
Cash flow available for financing activities					$681.0	$702.3	$722.7	$743.8	$765.6
Repurchase of equity					(415.5)	(434.9)	(455.6)	(477.4)	(500.4)
Dividends					(267.5)	(275.4)	(283.7)	(292.2)	(300.9)
Option proceeds					92.6	92.6	92.6	92.6	92.6
Plus: beginning cash balance					67.2	157.8	242.3	318.4	385.2
Less: minimum cash balance					(60.0)	(60.0)	(60.0)	(60.0)	(60.0)
Cash available for debt repayment					$97.8	$182.3	$258.4	$325.2	$382.0
Long-term debt issuance									
Long-term debt (repayment)									
Excess cash available for revolver									
Revolver									
Beginning balance									
Issuance / (repayment) of revolver									
Ending balance									
Long-term debt									
Beginning balance									
Issuance									
(Repayment)									
Ending balance									
Revolver	Average balances								
	Interest rate								
	Interest expense								
Long-term debt	Average balances								
	Interest rate								
	Interest expense								
	Total interest expense								
Cash	Average balances								
	Interest rate								
	Interest (income)								

References

Assumption

Calculations

Be Careful! Choose the correct column for the beginning cash balance

Reference the beginning cash balance from the balance sheet.
 – Remember, the beginning cash balance for one period is equal to the ending cash balance from the prior period (for example, the beginning cash balance on Proj 1 is equal to the ending cash balance on Hist 3).

Choose an assumption for the company's minimum cash balance (if any).
 – Companies typically keep a minimum amount of cash on hand to fund working capital requirements and daily cash payments. Look at historical cash balances: can you discern a trend?
 – Watch your signs: this amount should be negative since it will effectively reduce the cash flow available for debt repayment.

For now, skip long-term debt issuance/(repayment), excess cash available for the revolver, and the entire revolver section; these will be revisited later.

 Please view the Online Companion for related supplementary media.

	Fiscal Year Ending December 31,			Fiscal Year Ending December 31,				
	Hist 1	Hist 2	Hist 3	Proj 1	Proj 2	Proj 3	Proj 4	Proj 5
Cash flow available for financing activities				$681.0	$702.3	$722.7	$743.8	$765.6
Repurchase of equity				(415.5)	(434.9)	(455.6)	(477.4)	(500.4)
Dividends				(267.5)	(275.4)	(283.7)	(292.2)	(300.9)
Option proceeds				92.6	92.6	92.6	92.6	92.6
Plus: beginning cash balance				67.2	157.8	242.3	318.4	385.2
Less: minimum cash balance				(60.0)	(60.0)	(60.0)	(60.0)	(60.0)
Cash available for debt repayment				$97.8	$182.3	$258.4	$325.2	$382.0
Long-term debt issuance								
Long-term debt (repayment)								
Excess cash available for revolver								
Revolver								
Beginning balance								
Issuance / (repayment) of revolver								
Ending balance								
Long-term debt								
Beginning balance								
Issuance								
(Repayment)								
Ending balance	$969.0	$969.6	$1,680.5					

References →

Revolver	Average balances							
	Interest rate							
	Interest expense							
Long-term debt	Average balances							
	Interest rate							
	Interest expense							
	Total interest expense							
Cash	Average balances							
	Interest rate							
	Interest (income)							

Reference historical long-term debt balances from the balance sheet.

– Reference only ending balances here; the other information is not needed for historical periods.

NOTES ·····························

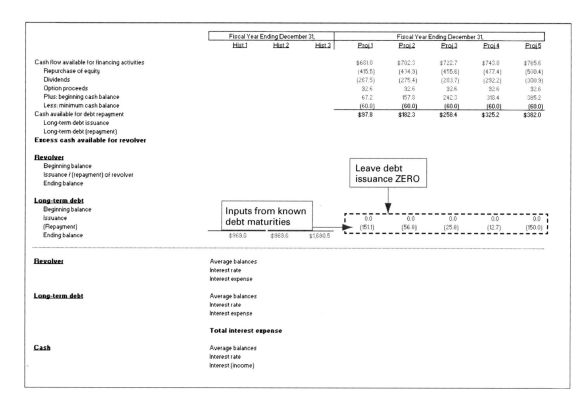

Input expected debt repayments in the repayment line.

- This data can usually be found in the long-term debt footnote of the company's latest 10-K or annual report.

- Companies typically list the aggregate amount of expected long-term debt repayments for the next few years.

- Alternatively, the various tranches of long-term debt may be broken-out individually and you will need to calculate aggregate amounts of debt repayments based on the maturities and principal amounts listed.

- Watch your signs: repayments should be negative since they will reduce the debt balance.

Input the expected debt issuance for the company.

- If information is available, it would likely appear in the long-term debt footnote or in a company press release.

- If no information is available, input zeroes throughout the projection period.

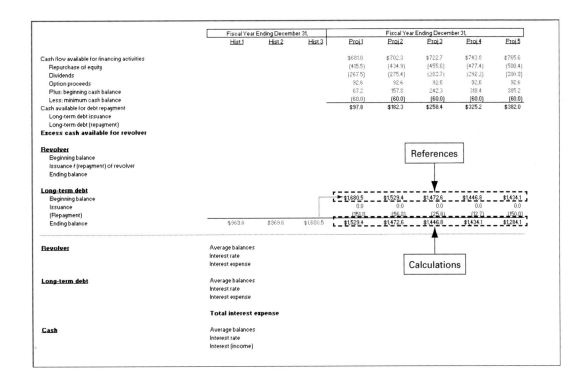

	Hist 1	Hist 2	Hist 3	Proj 1	Proj 2	Proj 3	Proj 4	Proj 5
Cash flow available for financing activities				$681.0	$702.3	$722.7	$743.8	$765.6
Repurchase of equity				(415.5)	(434.9)	(455.6)	(477.4)	(500.4)
Dividends				(267.5)	(275.4)	(283.7)	(292.2)	(300.9)
Option proceeds				92.6	92.6	92.6	92.6	92.6
Plus: beginning cash balance				67.2	157.8	242.3	318.4	385.2
Less: minimum cash balance				(60.0)	(60.0)	(60.0)	(60.0)	(60.0)
Cash available for debt repayment				$97.8	$182.3	$258.4	$325.2	$382.0
Long-term debt issuance								
Long-term debt (repayment)								
Excess cash available for revolver								
Revolver								
Beginning balance								
Issuance / (repayment) of revolver								
Ending balance								
Long-term debt								
Beginning balance				$1,680.5	$1,529.4	$1,472.6	$1,446.8	$1,434.1
Issuance				0.0	0.0	0.0	0.0	0.0
(Repayment)				(151.0)	(56.8)	(25.8)	(12.7)	(150.0)
Ending balance	$963.0	$969.6	$1,680.5	$1,529.4	$1,472.6	$1,446.8	$1,434.1	$1,284.1

References

Calculations

	Hist 1	Hist 2	Hist 3
Revolver			
Average balances			
Interest rate			
Interest expense			
Long-term debt			
Average balances			
Interest rate			
Interest expense			
Total interest expense			
Cash			
Average balances			
Interest rate			
Interest (income)			

Corkscrew the debt balance: link the beginning balance of the first projected period to the ending balance of the last historical period.

– Copy this formula to the right for all the projection periods.

Calculate the ending balance for each of the projected periods by summing the three line items above it.

 Please view the Online Companion for related supplementary media.

NOTES

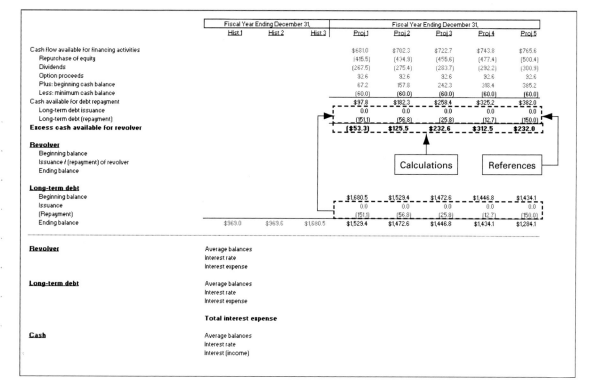

	Fiscal Year Ending December 31,			Fiscal Year Ending December 31,				
	Hist 1	Hist 2	Hist 3	Proj 1	Proj 2	Proj 3	Proj 4	Proj 5
Cash flow available for financing activities				$681.0	$702.3	$722.7	$743.8	$765.6
Repurchase of equity				(415.5)	(434.9)	(455.6)	(477.4)	(500.4)
Dividends				(267.5)	(275.4)	(283.7)	(292.2)	(300.9)
Option proceeds				92.6	92.6	92.6	92.6	92.6
Plus: beginning cash balance				67.2	157.8	242.3	318.4	385.2
Less: minimum cash balance				(60.0)	(60.0)	(60.0)	(60.0)	(60.0)
Cash available for debt repayment				$97.8	$182.3	$258.4	$325.2	$382.0
Long-term debt issuance				0.0	0.0	0.0	0.0	0.0
Long-term debt (repayment)				(151.1)	(56.8)	(25.8)	(12.7)	(150.0)
Excess cash available for revolver				**($53.3)**	**$125.5**	**$232.6**	**$312.5**	**$232.0**
Revolver								
Beginning balance								
Issuance / (repayment) of revolver								
Ending balance								
Long-term debt								
Beginning balance				$1,680.5	$1,529.4	$1,472.6	$1,446.8	$1,434.1
Issuance				0.0	0.0	0.0	0.0	0.0
(Repayment)				(151.1)	(56.8)	(25.8)	(12.7)	(150.0)
Ending balance	$969.0	$969.6	$1,680.5	$1,529.4	$1,472.6	$1,446.8	$1,434.1	$1,284.1

Calculations   References

Revolver	Average balances
	Interest rate
	Interest expense
Long-term debt	Average balances
	Interest rate
	Interest expense
	Total interest expense
Cash	Average balances
	Interest rate
	Interest (income)

Beneath cash available for debt repayment, which we calculated in Step 64, reference long-term debt issuance and long-term debt (repayment), that we created in Step 66.

Calculate excess cash available for the revolver by summing the lines cash available for debt repayment, long-term debt issuance, and long-term debt (repayment).

- Be careful when using the auto-sum function: it will miss the cash available for debt repayment line, so be sure to expand the range to capture this item.

	Fiscal Year Ending December 31,			Fiscal Year Ending December 31,				
	Hist 1	Hist 2	Hist 3	Proj 1	Proj 2	Proj 3	Proj 4	Proj 5
Cash flow available for financing activities				$681.0	$702.3	$722.7	$743.8	$765.6
Repurchase of equity				(415.5)	(434.9)	(455.6)	(477.4)	(500.4)
Dividends				(267.5)	(275.4)	(283.7)	(292.2)	(300.9)
Option proceeds				92.6	92.6	92.6	92.6	92.6
Plus: beginning cash balance				67.2	157.8	242.3	318.4	385.2
Less: minimum cash balance				(60.0)	(60.0)	(60.0)	(60.0)	(60.0)
Cash available for debt repayment				$97.8	$182.3	$258.4	$325.2	$382.0
Long-term debt issuance				0.0	0.0	0.0	0.0	0.0
Long-term debt (repayment)				(151.1)	(56.8)	(25.8)	(12.7)	(150.0)
Excess cash available for revolver				**($53.3)**	**$125.5**	**$232.6**	**$312.5**	**$232.0**
Revolver								
Beginning balance								
Issuance / (repayment) of revolver								
Ending balance	$12.0	$343.3	$814					
Long-term debt								
Beginning balance				$1,680.5	$1,529.4	$1,472.6	$1,446.8	$1,434.1
Issuance				0.0	0.0	0.0	0.0	0.0
(Repayment)				(151.1)	(56.8)	(25.8)	(12.7)	(150.0)
Ending balance	$369.0	$369.8	$1,680.5	$1,529.4	$1,472.6	$1,446.8	$1,434.1	$1,284.1
Revolver								
Average balances								
Interest rate								
Interest expense								
Long-term debt								
Average balances								
Interest rate								
Interest expense								
Total interest expense								
Cash								
Average balances								
Interest rate								
Interest (income)								

References →

Reference the revolver's historical ending balance from the balance sheet.

STEP 70

Set up the logic
for the revolver formula

The revolver in our model acts as a "cash sweep." If we build the revolver logic properly, then excess cash will be "swept up" and used to pay down the revolver balance. If there is a cash deficit (for example, cash is needed to fund working capital) the revolver will be drawn down (that is, borrowed against) to pay those bills.

– Remember that the revolver acts much like a credit card for the company.

If modeled properly, the revolver should be able to:

– Borrow cash if there is a deficit

– Pay itself down if there is excess cash available, and

– Stop paying itself down when its balance reaches zero (thereby accumulating cash on the balance sheet)

The MIN function provides an effective way to capture these various tasks.

– The MIN function compares a given set of numbers and returns the smallest number from the set (numbers listed in parenthesis, separated by commas). To model the revolver, build the following formula in Excel:

| = | – MIN x | (excess cash available for the revolver, beginning balance of the revolver) |

– If the excess cash available for the revolver is negative, it will be the smallest number and the company will need to borrow this amount.

– If the excess cash available for the revolver is positive, the company will be able to pay back the smaller of either the cash available or the beginning balance. Therefore, the company can't pay more than the cash available and won't pay back more than the beginning balance.

– It's important to remember the negative sign at the front of the equation. This ensures that the sign of the value returned to the cell represents an issuance (positive) or repayment (negative) as appropriate.

Please view the Online Companion for related supplementary media.

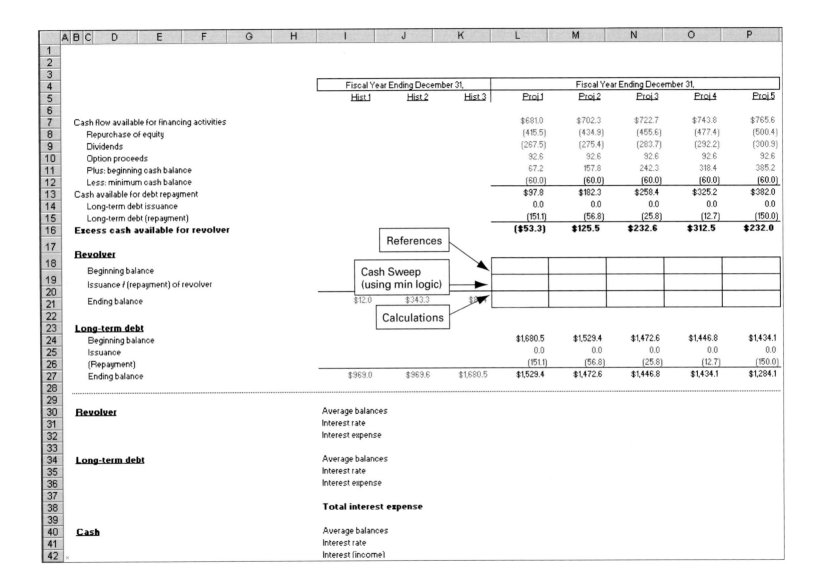

		Fiscal Year Ending December 31,			Fiscal Year Ending December 31,				
		Hist 1	Hist 2	Hist 3	Proj 1	Proj 2	Proj 3	Proj 4	Proj 5
Cash flow available for financing activities					$681.0	$702.3	$722.7	$743.8	$765.6
Repurchase of equity					(415.5)	(434.9)	(455.6)	(477.4)	(500.4)
Dividends					(267.5)	(275.4)	(283.7)	(292.2)	(300.9)
Option proceeds					92.6	92.6	92.6	92.6	92.6
Plus: beginning cash balance					67.2	157.8	242.3	318.4	385.2
Less: minimum cash balance					(60.0)	(60.0)	(60.0)	(60.0)	(60.0)
Cash available for debt repayment					$97.8	$182.3	$258.4	$325.2	$382.0
Long-term debt issuance					0.0	0.0	0.0	0.0	0.0
Long-term debt (repayment)					(151.1)	(56.8)	(25.8)	(12.7)	(150.0)
Excess cash available for revolver					**($53.3)**	**$125.5**	**$232.6**	**$312.5**	**$232.0**
Revolver									
Beginning balance									
Issuance / (repayment) of revolver									
Ending balance		$12.0	$343.3	$2??					
Long-term debt									
Beginning balance					$1,680.5	$1,529.4	$1,472.6	$1,446.8	$1,434.1
Issuance					0.0	0.0	0.0	0.0	0.0
(Repayment)					(151.1)	(56.8)	(25.8)	(12.7)	(150.0)
Ending balance		$969.0	$969.6	$1,680.5	$1,529.4	$1,472.6	$1,446.8	$1,434.1	$1,284.1
Revolver		Average balances							
		Interest rate							
		Interest expense							
Long-term debt		Average balances							
		Interest rate							
		Interest expense							
		Total interest expense							
Cash		Average balances							
		Interest rate							
		Interest (income)							

Callouts in the figure: References, Cash Sweep (using min logic), Calculations

NOTES

....

....

....

....

....

....

	Fiscal Year Ending December 31,			Fiscal Year Ending December 31,				
	Hist 1	Hist 2	Hist 3	Proj 1	Proj 2	Proj 3	Proj 4	Proj 5
Cash flow available for financing activities				$681.0	$702.3	$722.7	$743.8	$765.6
Repurchase of equity				(415.5)	(434.9)	(455.6)	(477.4)	(500.4)
Dividends				(267.5)	(275.4)	(283.7)	(292.2)	(300.9)
Option proceeds				92.6	92.6	92.6	92.6	92.6
Plus: beginning cash balance				67.2	157.8	242.3	318.4	395.2
Less: minimum cash balance				(60.0)	(60.0)	(60.0)	(60.0)	(60.0)
Cash available for debt repayment				$97.8	$182.3	$258.4	$325.2	$382.0
Long-term debt issuance				0.0	0.0	0.0	0.0	0.0
Long-term debt (repayment)				(151.1)	(56.8)	(25.8)	(12.7)	(150.0)
Excess cash available for revolver				**($53.3)**	**$125.5**	**$232.6**	**$312.5**	**$232.0**
Revolver								
Beginning balance				$81.4	$134.7	$9.1	$0.0	$0.0
Issuance / (repayment) of revolver				53.3	(125.5)	(9.1)	0.0	0.0
Ending balance	$12.0	$343.0	$81.4	$134.7	$9.1	$0.0	$0.0	$0.0
Long-term debt								
Beginning balance				$1,680.5	$1,529.4	$1,472.6	$1,446.8	$1,434.1
Issuance				0.0	0.0	0.0	0.0	0.0
(Repayment)				(151.1)	(56.8)	(25.8)	(12.7)	(150.0)
Ending balance	$969.0	$969.6	$1,680.5	$1,529.4	$1,472.6	$1,446.8	$1,434.1	$1,284.1
Revolver		Average balances		$108.0	$71.9	$4.6	$0.0	$0.0
		Interest rate		4.3%	4.3%	4.3%	4.3%	4.3%
		Interest expense		$4.6	$3.1	$0.2	$0.0	$0.0
Long-term debt		Average balances						
		Interest rate						
		Interest expense						
		Total interest expense						
Cash		Average balances						
		Interest rate						
		Interest (income)						

Assumption/Driver Calculations

Calculate the average balance for the revolver by taking the average of the beginning and ending balances for each projected period.

Make a reasonable assumption for an interest rate on the revolving credit facility.

- Look in the company filings or company-provided financial reports for disclosure on the interest rate the company pays on its revolver.
  - If it's disclosed, it will typically be found in a "revolving credit facility" or other financial footnote related to debt.
- You can keep this rate constant throughout the projection period, or make slight adjustments based on where you expect the credit markets to go.
  - Remember: choose something reasonable and defensible.

Calculate interest expense by multiplying average balances by the interest rate.

NOTES

Calculate the average balance for the long-term debt by taking the average of the beginning and ending balances for each projected period.

Make a reasonable assumption for a weighted average interest rate on the long-term debt.

- Look in the company filings or company-provided financial reports for disclosure on the interest rate the company pays on its long-term debt.

  - If it's disclosed, it will typically be found in a "long-term debt" or other financial footnote related to debt.

- If a weighted average interest rate is unavailable:

  - Calculate the effective interest rate for the last historical period by dividing gross interest expense (less any interest expense paid on the revolver) by the average balance of long-term debt.

  - Use the outstanding balances for each of the debt pieces listed in the debt footnote to calculate the weighted-average interest rate for long-term debt.

- You can keep this rate constant throughout the projection period, or make slight adjustments based on where you expect the credit markets to go.

  - Remember: choose something reasonable and defensible.

Calculate interest expense by multiplying average balances by the interest rate.

REFER TO SCREENSHOT ON THE RIGHT ⟶

	Fiscal Year Ending December 31,			Fiscal Year Ending December 31,				
	Hist 1	Hist 2	Hist 3	Proj 1	Proj 2	Proj 3	Proj 4	Proj 5
Cash flow available for financing activities				$681.0	$702.3	$722.7	$743.8	$765.6
Repurchase of equity				(415.5)	(434.9)	(455.6)	(477.4)	(500.4)
Dividends				(267.5)	(275.4)	(283.7)	(292.2)	(300.9)
Option proceeds				92.6	92.6	92.6	92.6	92.6
Plus: beginning cash balance				67.2	157.8	242.3	318.4	385.2
Less: minimum cash balance				(60.0)	(60.0)	(60.0)	(60.0)	(60.0)
Cash available for debt repayment				$97.8	$182.3	$258.4	$325.2	$382.0
Long-term debt issuance				0.0	0.0	0.0	0.0	0.0
Long-term debt (repayment)				(151.1)	(56.8)	(25.8)	(12.7)	(150.0)
Excess cash available for revolver				**($53.3)**	**$125.5**	**$232.6**	**$312.5**	**$232.0**
Revolver								
Beginning balance				$81.4	$134.7	$9.1	$0.0	$0.0
Issuance / (repayment) of revolver				53.3	(125.5)	(9.1)	0.0	0.0
Ending balance	$12.0	$343.3	$81.4	$134.7	$9.1	$0.0	$0.0	$0.0
Long-term debt								
Beginning balance				$1,680.5	$1,529.4	$1,472.6	$1,446.8	$1,434.1
Issuance				0.0	0.0	0.0	0.0	0.0
(Repayment)				(151.1)	(56.8)	(25.8)	(12.7)	(150.0)
Ending balance	$969.0	$969.6	$1,680.5	$1,529.4	$1,472.6	$1,446.8	$1,434.1	$1,284.1

		Proj 1	Proj 2	Proj 3	Proj 4	Proj 5	
Revolver	Average balances	$108.0	$71.9	$4.6	$0.0	$0.0	
	Interest rate	4.3%	4.3%	4.3%	4.3%	4.3%	0.0%
	Interest expense	$4.6	$3.1	$0.2	$0.0	$0.0	
Long-term debt	Average balances	$1,605.0	$1,501.0	$1,459.7	$1,440.5	$1,359.1	
	Interest rate	6.5%	6.5%	6.5%	6.5%	6.5%	
	Interest expense	$104.3	$97.6	$94.9	$93.6	$88.3	
	Total interest expense	**$109.0**	**$100.7**	**$95.1**	**$93.6**	**$88.3**	
Cash	Average balances						
	Interest rate						0.0%
	Interest (income)						

Assumption/Driver

Calculations

NOTES

Calculate the average cash balance by taking the average of the beginning and ending balances for each projected period from the balance sheet.

– Be careful with your references here. For example, calculating the average cash balance for Proj 1 requires linking to ending cash balances for Hist 3 and Proj 1, not Proj 1 and Proj 2.

Make a reasonable assumption for an interest rate on the cash balance.

– There are a couple of options here:

– Assume a small, reasonable interest rate on cash balances, for example, 1.0%.

– Calculate the effective interest rate for the last historical period by dividing the interest income from the income statement by the average cash balance for the period.

– You can keep this rate constant throughout the projection period, or make slight adjustments based on where you expect the credit markets to go.

– Remember: choose something reasonable and defensible.

Calculate interest income by multiplying average balances by the interest rate.

– Careful with your signs: interest income should be negative because it deducts from interest expense and is reflected as a negative on the income statement.

REFER TO SCREENSHOT ON THE RIGHT ⟶

 Please view the Online Companion for related supplementary media.

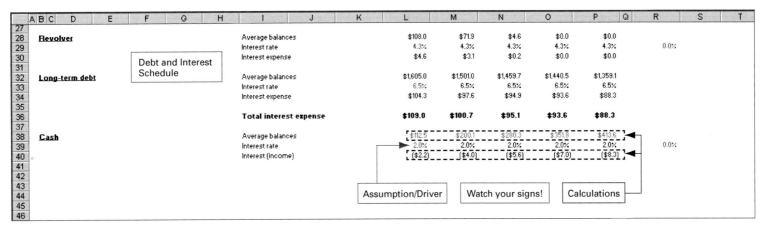

Debt and Interest Schedule

	L	M	N	O	P	Q
Revolver						
Average balances	$108.0	$71.9	$4.6	$0.0	$0.0	
Interest rate	4.3%	4.3%	4.3%	4.3%	4.3%	0.0%
Interest expense	$4.6	$3.1	$0.2	$0.0	$0.0	
Long-term debt						
Average balances	$1,605.0	$1,501.0	$1,459.7	$1,440.5	$1,359.1	
Interest rate	6.5%	6.5%	6.5%	6.5%	6.5%	
Interest expense	$104.3	$97.6	$94.9	$93.6	$88.3	
Total interest expense	**$109.0**	**$100.7**	**$95.1**	**$93.6**	**$88.3**	
Cash						
Average balances	$112.5	$200.1	$280.3	$351.8	$413.6	
Interest rate	2.0%	2.0%	2.0%	2.0%	2.0%	0.0%
Interest (income)	($2.2)	($4.0)	($5.6)	($7.0)	($8.3)	

Assumption/Driver   Watch your signs!   Calculations

Balance Sheet

	Fiscal Year Ending December 31,			Fiscal Year Ending December 31,				
	Hist 1	Hist 2	Hist 3	Proj 1	Proj 2	Proj 3	Proj 4	Proj 5
Cash	$114.8	$54.8	$67.2	$157.8	$242.3	$318.4	$385.2	$442.0
Accounts receivable, net	407.6	408.9	559.3	573.2	590.4	608.1	626.3	645.1
Inventories	492.9	557.2	610.3	626.2	645.0	664.3	684.2	704.8
Other current assets	116.3	176.7	172.2	179.3	184.7	190.2	195.9	201.8
Total current assets	1,131.6	1,197.7	1,408.9					

NOTES

			Fiscal Year Ending December 31,			Fiscal Year Ending December 31,				
			Hist 1	Hist 2	Hist 3	Proj 1	Proj 2	Proj 3	Proj 4	Proj 5
5	Cash flow available for financing activities					$681.0	$702.3	$722.7	$743.8	$765.6
6	Repurchase of equity					(415.5)	(434.9)	(455.6)	(477.4)	(500.4)
7	Dividends					(267.5)	(275.4)	(283.7)	(292.2)	(300.9)
8	Option proceeds					92.6	92.6	92.6	92.6	92.6
9	Plus: beginning cash balance					87.2	157.3	242.3	318.4	385.2
10	Less: minimum cash balance					(60.0)	(60.0)	(60.0)	(60.0)	(60.0)
11	Cash available for debt repayment					$97.8	$182.3	$258.4	$325.2	$382.0
12	Long-term debt issuance					0.0	0.0	0.0	0.0	0.0
13	Long-term debt (repayment)					(151.1)	(56.8)	(25.8)	(12.7)	(150.0)
14	**Excess cash available for revolver**					**($53.3)**	**$125.5**	**$232.6**	**$312.5**	**$232.0**
16	**Revolver**									
17	Beginning balance					$81.4	$134.7	$9.1	$0.0	$0.0
18	Issuance / (repayment) of revolver					53.3	(125.5)	(9.1)	0.0	0.0
19	Ending balance		$12.0	$343.3	$81.4	$134.7	$9.1	$0.0	$0.0	$0.0
21	**Long-term debt**									
22	Beginning balance					$1,680.5	$1,529.4	$1,472.6	$1,446.8	$1,434.1
23	Issuance					0.0	0.0	0.0	0.0	0.0
24	(Repayment)					(151.1)	(56.8)	(25.8)	(12.7)	(150.0)
25	Ending balance		$969.0	$969.6	$1,680.5	$1,529.4	$1,472.6	$1,446.8	$1,434.1	$1,284.1
28	**Revolver**		Average balances			$108.0	$71.9	$4.6	$0.0	$0.0
29			Interest rate			4.3%	4.3%	4.3%	4.3%	4.3%
30			Interest expense			$4.6	$3.1	$0.2	$0.0	$0.0
32	**Long-term debt**		Average balances			$1,605.0	$1,501.0	$1,459.7	$1,440.5	$1,359.1
33			Interest rate			6.5%	6.5%	6.5%	6.5%	6.5%
34			Interest expense			$104.3	$97.6	$94.9	$93.6	$88.3
36			**Total interest expense**			**$109.0**	**$100.7**	**$95.1**	**$93.6**	**$88.3**
38	**Cash**		Average balances			$112.5	$200.1	$280.3	$351.8	$413.6
39			Interest rate			2.0%	2.0%	2.0%	2.0%	2.0%
40			Interest (income)			($2.2)	($4.0)	($5.6)	($7.0)	($8.3)

> Right border on the last historical year as a "divider." Make this the **LAST** thing you do on the schedule!

NOTES

STEP 74

Link debt repayments and issuances to the cash flow statement

NOTES

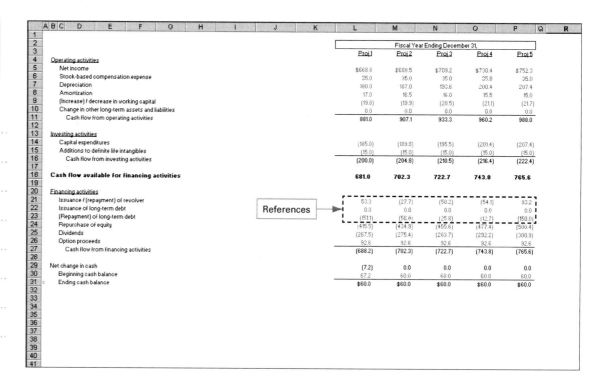

Reference the first three lines of the financing activities section (issuance/(repayment) of the revolver, issuance of long-term debt, and (repayment) of long-term debt) from the debt and interest schedule.

- Be careful with your signs: issuances should be positive because they represent cash inflows, and repayments should be negative because they represent cash outflows.

	Fiscal Year Ending December 31,			Fiscal Year Ending December 31,				
	Hist 1	Hist 2	Hist 3	Proj 1	Proj 2	Proj 3	Proj 4	Proj 5
Cash	$114.8	$54.8	$67.2	$60.0	$60.0	$60.0	$60.0	$60.0
Accounts receivable, net	407.6	408.9	559.3	573.2	590.4	608.1	626.3	645.1
Inventories	492.9	557.2	610.3	626.2	645.0	664.3	684.2	704.8
Other current assets	116.3	176.7	172.2	179.3	184.7	190.2	195.9	201.8
Total current assets	1,131.6	1,197.7	1,408.9	1,438.7	1,480.0	1,522.6	1,566.5	1,611.7
PP&E, net	1,661.9	1,682.7	1,853.1	1,864.1	1,667.0	1,668.9	1,669.9	1,669.9
Definite life intangibles	46.2	61.0	65.1	63.1	61.6	60.6	60.1	60.1
Indefinite life intangibles	31.6	100.3	111.9	111.9	111.9	111.9	111.9	111.9
Goodwill	389.0	463.9	487.3	487.3	487.3	487.3	487.3	487.3
Other long-term assets	322.3	307.1	562.8	562.8	562.8	562.8	562.8	562.8
Total assets	**$3,582.5**	**$3,812.8**	**$4,295.2**	**$4,328.0**	**$4,370.7**	**$4,414.2**	**$4,458.6**	**$4,503.8**
Accounts payable	$132.2	$148.7	$167.8	$171.1	$176.3	$181.6	$187.0	$192.6
Accrued liabilities	416.2	469.2	507.8	522.4	538.1	554.2	570.9	588.0
Other current liabilities	24.9	42.3	23.5	22.7	23.4	24.1	24.8	25.6
Total current liabilities	573.3	660.2	699.1	716.3	737.7	759.9	782.7	806.2
Revolver	12.0	343.3	81.4	134.7	106.9	56.7	2.6	95.8
Long-term debt	969.0	969.6	1,680.5	1,529.4	1,472.6	1,446.8	1,434.1	1,284.1
Deferred income taxes	377.6	319.2	400.3	400.3	400.3	400.3	400.3	400.3
Other long-term liabilities	370.8	383.4	412.9	412.9	412.9	412.9	412.9	412.9
Total liabilities	2,302.7	2,675.7	3,274.2	3,193.5	3,130.5	3,076.6	3,032.6	2,999.2
Total equity	1,279.9	1,137.1	1,021.1	1,134.4	1,240.2	1,337.6	1,426.0	1,504.6
Total liabilities and equity	**$3,582.5**	**$3,812.8**	**$4,295.2**	**$4,328.0**	**$4,370.7**	**$4,414.2**	**$4,458.6**	**$4,503.8**
Parity check (A=L+E)	0.000	0.000	0.000	0.000	0.000	0.000	0.000	0.000

Right border on the last historical year as a "divider." Make this the **LAST** thing you do on the schedule!

References

Calculations

NOTES

Link the projected revolver and long-term debt balances to their respective lines on the balance sheet.

Calculate total current assets, total assets, total current liabilities, total liabilities, and total liabilities and equity.

– Be careful! Make sure the total assets and total liabilities calculations include current assets and current liabilities.

Add in the 'Parity Check.' This check tests whether assets equal liabilities plus equity (A = L + E).

– This formula is equivalent to Total Assets – (Total Liabilities and Equity).

– If the model is balanced, then the cells on this line should read zero for every historical and projected period.

Please view the Online Companion for related supplementary media.

NOTES

		Fiscal Year Ending December 31,			Fiscal Year Ending December 31,					5 Year CAGR
		Hist 1	Hist 2	Hist 3	Proj 1	Proj 2	Proj 3	Proj 4	Proj 5	
Sales		$4,172.6	$4,429.2	$4,836.0	$4,981.1	$5,130.5	$5,284.4	$5,442.9	$5,606.2	3.0%
Cost of goods sold, excluding depreciation (1)		2,383.7	2,509.2	2,764.7	2,839.2	2,924.4	3,012.1	3,102.5	3,195.5	
Gross profit		1,788.9	1,920.0	2,071.2	2,141.9	2,206.1	2,272.3	2,340.5	2,410.7	3.1%
SG&A expenses, excluding am		819.5	848.7	895.1	896.6	923.5	951.2	979.7	1,009.1	
Other operating (income) / exp		0.0	0.0	0.0	0.0	0.0	0.0	0.0	0.0	
EBITDA		969.4	1,071.4	1,176.1	1,245.3	1,282.6	1,321.1	1,360.7	1,401.6	3.6%
Depreciation (1)		158.9	171.2	178.3	180.0	187.0	193.6	200.4	207.4	
Amortization		21.6	18.4	17.9	17.0	16.5	16.0	15.5	15.0	
EBIT (2)		788.8	881.7	979.9	1,048.3	1,079.1	1,111.5	1,144.9	1,179.1	3.8%
Interest expense		65.3	67.9	89.5	108.9	102.7	98.2	94.7	90.1	
Interest (income)		(1.7)	(1.4)	(1.5)	(1.3)	(1.2)	(1.2)	(1.3)	(1.3)	
Other non-operating (income) / expense		0.0	0.0	0.0	0.0	0.0	0.0	0.0	0.0	
Pretax income		725.3	815.2	891.9	940.6	977.7	1,014.5	1,051.4	1,090.3	4.1%
Income taxes (3)		266.2	298.4	324.7	340.5	353.9	367.3	380.6		
Net income (4)		**$459.1**	**$516.8**	**$567.3**	**$600.1**	**$623.8**	**$647.3**	**$670.8**		4.2%
Diluted weighted average shares in millions		264.532	256.934	248.292	242.248	238.248	234.248	230.248	226.248	(1.8%)
Earnings per share		**$1.74**	**$2.01**	**$2.28**	**$2.48**	**$2.62**	**$2.76**	**$2.91**	**$3.07**	6.1%
Ratios & assumptions										
Sales growth rate			6.2%	9.2%	3.0%	3.0%	3.0%	3.0%	3.0%	
Gross margin		42.9%	43.3%	42.8%	43.0%	43.0%	43.0%	43.0%	43.0%	
SG&A expenses (as a % of sales)		19.6%	19.2%	18.5%	18.0%	18.0%	18.0%	18.0%	18.0%	
Other operating (income) / expenses ($ amount)		$0.0	$0.0	$0.0	$0.0	$0.0	$0.0	$0.0	$0.0	
Other non-operating (income) / expense ($ amount)		0.0	0.0	0.0	0.0	0.0	0.0	0.0	0.0	
Effective tax rate		36.7%	36.6%	36.4%	36.2%	36.2%	36.2%	36.2%	36.2%	

Right border on the last historical year as a "divider." Make this the **LAST** thing you do on the schedule!

References

Question:
– What impact will linking these numbers have on your model?

Answer:
– The answer will be discussed in the next part of the book!

Link projected interest expense and interest (income) to the income statement.

– Remember: interest income should be negative.

This step will make your model circular (please see 5.1 for a discussion of circularity). If you get an error stating that Excel cannot calculate a circular reference, follow the steps in the supplementary media.

 Please view the Online Companion for related supplementary media.

Iterative Debt and Interest Schedule

	Fiscal Year Ending December 31,			Fiscal Year Ending December 31,				
	Hist 1	Hist 2	Hist 3	Proj 1	Proj 2	Proj 3	Proj 4	Proj 5
Cash flow available for financing activities				$631.0	$702.3	$722.7	$743.8	$765.5
Repurchase of equity				(415.5)	(434.9)	(455.8)	(477.4)	(500.4)
Dividends				(267.5)	(275.4)	(283.7)	(292.2)	(300.9)
Option proceeds				92.6	92.6	92.6	92.6	92.6
Plus: beginning cash balance				67.2	60.0	60.0	60.0	60.0
Less: minimum cash balance				(60.0)	(60.0)	(60.0)	(60.0)	(60.0)
Cash available for debt repayment				$97.8	$84.5	$76.0	$66.8	$56.8
Long-term debt issuance				0.0	0.0	0.0	0.0	0.0
Long-term debt (repayment)				(151.1)	(56.8)	(25.8)	(12.7)	(150.0)
Excess cash available for revolver				**($53.3)**	**$27.7**	**$50.2**	**$54.1**	**($93.2)**
Revolver								
Beginning balance				$81.4	$134.7	$106.9	$56.7	$2.6
Issuance / (repayment) of revolver				53.3	(27.7)	(50.2)	(54.1)	93.2
Ending balance	$12.0	$343.3	$81.4	$134.7	$106.9	$56.7	$2.6	$95.8

D&I Schedule **BEFORE** linking interest expense and interest income to IS

	Fiscal Year Ending December 31,			Fiscal Year Ending December 31,				
	Hist 1	Hist 2	Hist 3	Proj 1	Proj 2	Proj 3	Proj 4	Proj 5
Cash flow available for financing activities				$612.3	$637.5	$660.9	$684.2	$708.9
Repurchase of equity				(372.8)	(394.0)	(415.9)	(438.5)	(462.7)
Dividends				(240.0)	(249.5)	(258.9)	(268.3)	(278.2)
Option proceeds				92.6	92.6	92.6	92.6	92.6
Plus: beginning cash balance				67.2	60.0	60.0	60.0	66.7
Less: minimum cash balance				(60.0)	(60.0)	(60.0)	(60.0)	(60.0)
Cash available for debt repayment				$99.2	$86.6	$78.7	$70.0	$67.3
Long-term debt issuance				0.0	0.0	0.0	0.0	0.0
Long-term debt (repayment)				(151.1)	(56.8)	(25.8)	(12.7)	(150.0)
Excess cash available for revolver				**($51.9)**	**$29.8**	**$52.9**	**$57.3**	**($82.7)**
Revolver								
Beginning balance				$81.4	$133.2	$103.4	$50.6	$0.0
Issuance / (repayment) of revolver				51.9	(29.8)	(52.9)	(50.6)	82.7
Ending balance	$12.0	$343.3	$81.4	$133.2	$103.4	$50.6	$0.0	$82.7

D&I Schedule **AFTER** linking interest expense and interest income to IS

Flow-of-funds

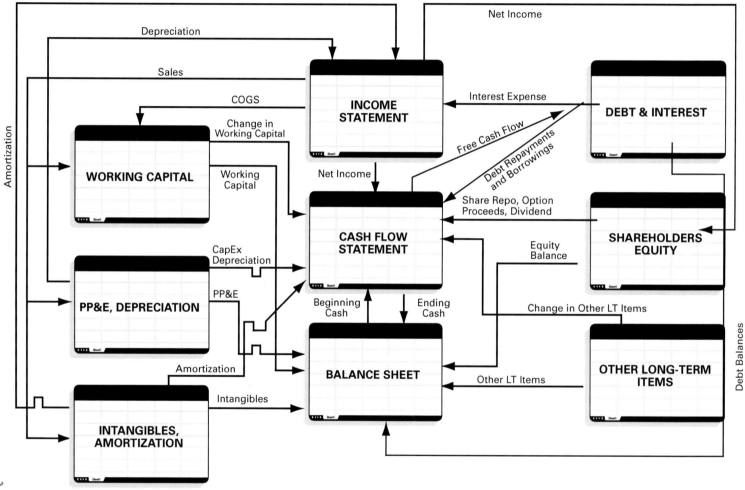

 Please view the Online Companion for related supplementary media.

Finishing Touches

Now that you've completed the steps for building your model, it is tempting to believe that you are done. It is at this stage, however, that an experienced modeler realizes their work is, in a sense, really just beginning. In the remaining sections of this guide, we will discuss techniques for troubleshooting your 'finished' model to make sure it is truly in working condition.

Next, we will explore applications of the finished product to answer a fundamental question: What can I actually *do* with this completed financial model? How can I apply it to solve the everyday problems and challenges I'm faced with as a financial practitioner?

Keep in mind that some of the concepts we are about to cover are somewhat advanced; they may take additional study and practice to truly understand and master. Our goal is to give you a working knowledge of the approach proficient modelers take to 'finish' their models and put them to practical use.

Let's begin with troubleshooting your model.

 Please view the Online Companion for related supplementary media.

5.1 TROUBLESHOOTING YOUR MODEL

The Three Safety Checks

Before you can consider your model fully functional and ready to be used, there are a number of safety checks that you need to apply to it. Let's explore three of these safety checks, outlined below:

1. **Circularity check** – Your completed model is 'circular.' It is important to understand what circularity is and how to 'jump start' a circular model that is broken, or that has 'blown up.'

2. **Parity check** – A fully functional model must be balanced, or 'in parity.' That is, assets must equal the sum of liabilities and equity on the balance sheet (**A = L + E**).

3. **Check for 'deal' readiness** – Once you are satisfied that your circular model is functioning properly and is balanced, look it over again to ensure it is truly ready for a deal, for client presentation, or for some other similarly 'mission-critical' purpose.

I. The Circularity Check

When you calculated *interest expense* and linked it to the income statement **on step 76**, you created what is called a 'circular reference.' Excel defines a circular reference as a formula that "refers back to its own cell, either directly or indirectly." This is important because the program cannot calculate such a formula on its own. That is, circular references cannot be calculated automatically using Excel's default settings. **In a moment, we will expand our discussion of iterations and how to activate them in Excel.**

For now, just understand that because our model is circular, Excel has difficulty calculating a solution.

Exhibit 5.1

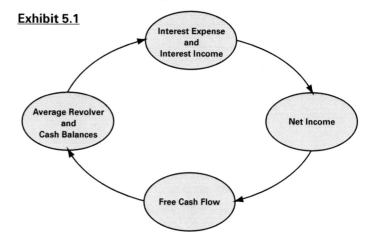

Before we describe how to calculate formulas in a circular model, let's pause here and first explain why your model is circular. The above diagram (Exhibit 5.1) illustrates how your model connects the income statement to the cash flow statement, the cash flow statement to the debt and interest schedule, and the debt and interest schedule back to the income statement in a circular way: As an example of circularity in your current model, let's say that in a given year the company you are modeling has a financing 'need' or cash flow 'deficit.' That is, it needs more cash to fund its operations, investments, and scheduled debt payments than it is currently generating. In such a scenario, your model's 'cash sweep' logic causes the revolver to kick in, or be 'drawn down,' generating increased short-term borrowings. If your company borrows more, then it will pay more interest expense. If it pays more in interest expense, then its net income will decrease. If its net income decreases, then its free cash flow will decrease, causing the original financing 'need' to become even greater. The vicious circle pattern continues indefinitely! As you can see, a circular model behaves much like a dog chasing its own tail.

It is exactly because of this infinite chain of connectivity that Excel cannot determine a solution—at least not on its own. To enable Excel to calculate in a circular model, you need to allow it to 'iterate' toward a solution. To switch on Excel's iteration functionality, navigate to the options menu:

Excel 2007: Office Button > Excel Options > Formulas or hotkey [ALT] , , , , , **Alt F I F, Alt+I**

Excel 2010/2013: File Tab > Options > Formula or hotkey [ALT] , , , , , **Alt F T F, Alt+I**

then activate the iterations function by putting a check in the Iterations box.

Exhibit 5.2

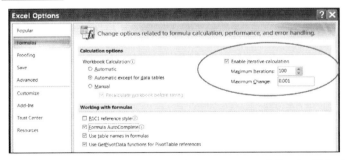

Excel 2007 environment displayed. Other versions of Excel will look slightly different.

Iterations can be a difficult concept to grasp. Essentially, Excel is performing a controlled number of iterative trials—or if you like, successive approximations or guesses—in an attempt to converge on, or arrive at, an answer. For calculus students, think of Excel's iterative functionality as an application of the limit convergence theory. For non-math types, the key point is this: for Excel to perform optimally within a circular model, its iterations functions must be switched on.

Can this functionality be fine-tuned? To a degree, yes. During our live training seminars, participants often discover that they can modify certain parameters within Excel's iterations functionality, such as the number of iterations. A fair question would be, "Does increasing the number of iterations improve the result of my model?" It can, but there is a trade-off: Increasing the number of iterations may increase the precision of your model (that is, allow Excel to get closer to the right answer), but it will also consume more of your computer's memory and processing power, perhaps needlessly. For this reason, we generally advise against entering a large number of iterations (for example, in the couple of thousands or larger).

The question to ask when choosing the number of iterations is: How complicated is the model I am working on? The answer should determine how many iterations Excel needs in order to converge on an answer. This is a somewhat open-ended question. We encourage you to seek internal resources for guidance in answering it (for example, from people who have worked on models similar to yours).

From our experience, Excel's default setting of 100 iterations should satisfy the level of precision typically required for the type of model we have built together. Nevertheless, if you're operating in this default setting mode, you can easily run additional iterations by pressing the F9 key on your keyboard; this action will prompt Excel to re-calculate your model by running an additional 100 iterations.

🖰 **Please view the Online Companion for related supplementary media.**

Errors with Circular Models and Jump Starting

Although circularity is a prerequisite to building a fully integrated financial model in Excel, it does introduce an element of risk to the process. The danger is barely noticeable when things are working fine. However, when an error is made, the weakness of a circular model is fully revealed. For example, you make an error while inputting a company's interest rate on debt (for example, perhaps the letter "o" is inputted when the number "0" was intended). Excel will crash or 'blow up' your model because the error gets trapped in the never-ending loop connecting interest expense, net income, and free cash flow, and never has an opportunity to correct itself.

When you make this type of error, Excel posts "#VALUE" messages in the affected cells. Here is a list of commonly occuring errors:

#VALUE: A cell reference to a letter rather than a number (as in the example above).

#REF: A reference to a cell that no longer exists (usually caused by deleting a cell, column, or row).

#DIV: An equation with zero in the denominator, or a blank cell.

#NAME: A reference to a name that does not exist (usually caused by deleting a name).

To fix a crashed model, you must '**jump-start**' it. Jump-starting prevents an error from flowing through your model by temporarily 'cutting' its circularity. With the never-ending loop put on 'pause,' you now have a chance to fix the error and the model has a chance to process the correct numbers. Once the model is fixed, circularity is restored and the model can begin functioning normally again.

Here is a 5-step method for jump-starting a blown-up model:

1) **Fix the error.** This may seem obvious, but it is a crucial first step that's often overlooked. The original error must be resolved before the jump-starting technique can take effect. In our example above, this would mean replacing the letter "o" with the intended number "0."

2) **On the income statement, <u>copy</u> the formulas for *interest expense* and *interest income* on the income statement.**

3) **Paste the copied formulas off to the right, beyond the last column of projections.**

4) **Delete the original *interest expense* and *interest income* formulas.** This step effectively 'zeros out,' or breaks, the model's circularity.

5) **Copy the *interest expense* and *interest income* formulas (which you pasted off to the right in step 3), and paste them back onto the income statement.** This step restores the model's circularity; the jump-start is now complete, and the model should be working properly again.

There is actually a quicker way to jump-start a model, which we have outlined below. This abbreviated version simply deletes then replaces the *interest expense* and *interest income* formulas, rather than copying and pasting them off to the side, effectively bypassing steps two and three:

1) **Fix the error.**

2) **Delete the original *interest expense* and *interest income* formulas.**

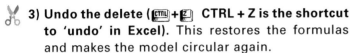 3) **Undo the delete (CTRL + Z is the shortcut to 'undo' in Excel).** This restores the formulas and makes the model circular again.

So why ever use the longer method? Bear in mind that the purpose of steps two and three in the 5-step method for jump-starting is to prevent you from losing the original *interest expense* and *interest income* formulas. In other words, we placed these formulas off to the right for safe-keeping. Why act so cautiously? Prudence. In our experience, many things can go wrong while you're in the middle of trying to fix a broken model. What if right after you delete these formulas, you receive a phone call or are whisked away to an emergency meeting before you can replace them? You may not remember to replace the formulas when you return to your desk hours later. Or, what if your auto-save feature is enabled, causing Excel to save after you've deleted your formulas? CTRL + Z will not undo the delete in this case. Excel cannot undo actions that occurred prior to a file being saved.

In short, steps two and three in the 5-step method protect against these and other unforeseen scenarios. In fact, it is a pretty good idea (and a modeling best practice) to take such precautions when you want to replace or change any important formulas in your model, not just the ones that cause circular references.

We focus on *interest expense* and *interest income* in jump-starting our model because these particular line items represent the vital link, or bridge, between the income statement and the cash flow statement. Without *interest expense* and *interest income*, the model would not be circular. In other words, these line items represent the point of circularity in our model which we must temporarily 'break' before restoring again. With practice, this concept will become second nature, and you can apply the abbreviated version of the jump-starting technique with confidence.

Keep in mind, however, that different models are circular for different reasons. For example, an LBO (leveraged buyout) model might be circular because of the way it calculates interest expense, similar to the model we have built. However, the same model could be circular for additional reasons, such as the way it calculates financing fees. In the example below, financing fees are calculated based on the amount of the deal being financed, which depends on the size of the deal, which in turn depends on the financing fees, thus completing the circular logic:

Exhibit 5.3

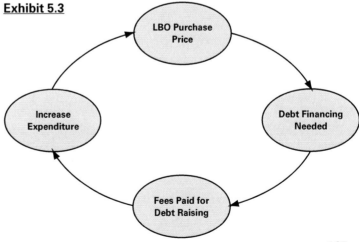

MODELING TIP

Some practitioners actually work in Excel with iterations turned off. The reason is that it gives them a way to identify which steps cause circularity. Once they perform a step where circular errors start occurring, that tells them that this step is one of the causes of circularity and a possible candidate for jump-starting. But this technique is useful only for finding the first circular spot in your model. Afterwards, you must have iterations turned on in order to calculate.

The goal of an effective modeler, therefore, is not simply to know that an LBO or any other model is circular, but rather, to know why (or more importantly, where) a model's circularity exists. Depending on a model's particular complexity and function, you may have to jump-start it simultaneously at multiple points.

Again, understanding these concepts comes from practice. Your goal here is to have a working knowledge of circularity and the challenges it presents. As you build models that meet the varying challenges of your work, we strongly suggest you seek other resources as needed.

Please view the Online Companion for related supplementary media.

II. The Parity Check: Checking for Balance

Let's move to the second of the three safety checks that we mentioned at the beginning of Section 5.1. The second check is to make sure your model is 'in parity,' or is balanced. This means that for every period in your model, both historical and forecasted, the value of assets on your balance sheet must equal the sum of liabilities and shareholders' equity ($A = L +$

E). In the model we built together, there is a 'parity check line' on the balance sheet designed exclusively for this reason. It is a basic formula that subtracts the sum of *liabilities* and *equity* from *assets*. For any given year, if the result of the calculation in the parity check line is zero, then the model is balanced.

Exhibit 5.4 shows a model that is in balance historically. Notice that the parity check line reads '0.000' in all historical years. The model goes out of balance beginning in the first projected year.

Exhibit 5.4

	Fiscal Year Ending December 31,			Fiscal Year Ending December 31,				
	Hist 1	Hist 2	Hist 3	Proj 1	Proj 2	Proj 3	Proj 4	Proj 5
Total liabilities and equity	$3,582.5	$3,812.8	$4,295.2	$4,194.7	$4,194.7	$4,194.7	$4,194.7	$4,194.7
Parity check (A=L+E)	0.000	0.000	0.000	370.000	370.000	370.000	370.000	370.000

Before exploring methods for balancing, we must first point out that balancing models is a technique that relies heavily on experience. It is not a skill that can be picked up overnight. The only way to gain expertise and efficiency in balancing models is through extensive practice in both building and troubleshooting models. That said, here are several tools to get you started.

The first of these tools is what we call the "5-minute test." This is essentially a series of quick checks designed to catch common errors. The approach here is to look first for the low-hanging fruit. If there aren't any (that is, if the 5-minute test doesn't work), then there is always the "brute force" method, which we'll describe next.

The 5-minute test:

- Make sure your historicals are balanced (i.e., **A = L + E** in all historical periods). If your historicals are not balanced, it is most likely a data entry error. Go back and check the source of your historical information to make sure that everything is entered in correctly. Also, go back and check your formulas to make sure that they are calculating correctly.

- Perform a quick sanity check on your balance sheet and cash flow statement:

  - Check cash flow items for possible incorrect signs (for example, depreciation should be <u>positive</u>; capital expenditures should be <u>negative</u>);

  - Look for unreasonable changes in balance sheet values between the first year you are in parity and the first year you are out of parity. An example would be if *property, plant, and equipment* have been around $500 million historically, then suddenly jumps to $1,000 million in a given year).

- Divide the amount of the error by two.

  - Usually sign errors get doubled: if a single sign error is the issue (for example, amortization is being subtracted rather than added back to net income on the cash flow statement), dividing by two isolates the error and helps target your search.

- Look for a consistent trend in the error.

  - Is the error growing by a constant amount? If so, there may be an omission of an item for all projected years.

  - Is the error amount the same in every year? If so, your error may occur only in the first year out of parity. Once you fix it, the following years should balance.

- Have you correctly linked items to or from other schedules?

  - For example, balance sheet items (for example, cash) should be linked to other schedules based on <u>ending balances</u>, not beginning balances (that is, this year's beginning balance should equal last year's ending balance).

- Check total formulas and other calculations.

If the 5-minute test does not catch your parity error, then unfortunately you will have to perform what we call the "brute force" method. Recall that a model is considered to be in parity when changes in the balance sheet can be reconciled by changes on the cash flow statement. The brute force method requires verifying this relationship by hand-checking the calculation of these changes, one by one.

Here is how to do it: We suggest printing out a copy of both the balance sheet and the cash flow statement. Then, using pen and paper (and a calculator), reconcile the changes in each and every balance sheet account with the corresponding events, or 'flows,' on the cash flow statement.

The following example illustrates how one would reconcile changes in the property, plant, and equipment account with the corresponding flows (that is, depreciation and capital expenditures) on the cash flow statement:

Exhibit 5.5

PP&E, net

Balance Sheet				Cash Flow		
Beginning Bal.	Ending Bal.	**Difference**		Depr.	CapEx	**Total**
1,659.138	1,664.138	**(5.000)**		180.000	(185.000)	**(5.000)**

The change in the PP&E account on the balance sheet ($5 million net increase) reconciles with the corresponding depreciation and capital expenditures on the cash flow statement ($5 million net cash outflow). That tells you that this is not the source of your error, and it is time to keep looking. Work downward on your balance sheet, hand-checking year-over-year changes in each account with the appropriate corresponding cash flow(s) as you go.

The brute force method takes time and patience, but is a surefire way to spot the source of your parity error when all else fails. Here is where the value of stress-testing becomes abundantly clear. By verifying the logic of your formulas and the accuracy of your links along the way, you can keep track of the flow-of-funds as you build the model, rather than waiting until the end to uncover a potentially big problem. Stress-testing therefore minimizes the chance that your model will be out of balance or require brute force correction upon completion.

Please view the Online Companion for related supplementary media.

III. Checking for Deal Readiness

In form and function, the model we completed together is similar to the models used by financial professionals in actual deals. Whatever a model's purpose, making it "deal ready" is an important last step. A deal-ready model is one that is presentable internally (that is, to your boss or peers in a deal team) and/or externally (that is, to a potential or existing client). In other words, a model is considered deal ready if it is ready to be used in a real-world situation. There are several important sub-checks to ensure a model is deal-ready:

1) It is in parity or balanced;

2) Its assumptions are reasonable and defensible;

3) Its worksheets, especially output pages, are properly formatted;

4) Important inputs, especially assumptions, are properly footnoted; and

5) Every single calculation has been checked by hand.

Keep in mind that a balanced, functional model is not necessarily 'correct.' You must also be confident in the supporting story behind the numbers. We will explore this concept next in our discussion below.

 Please view the Online Companion for related supplementary media.

5.2 THE FINISHED PRODUCT

You are almost done! The heavy lifting is over, but there is still a little more work to be done. The final section of this book explores applications of your completed model and how to transform it into a finished product.

Some Caveats Regarding the Model

A theme we have emphasized throughout this process is that there isn't a single, correct way to build a model. Similarly, there is no universal model to serve all purposes. For that reason, you should understand certain limitations to our model and be prepared to make adjustments to match your particular purposes. Here are four key caveats:

I. This is an annual model—it ignores seasonality.

Seasonality can be defined as the somewhat predictable variations in sales patterns throughout a fiscal year. These variations can be driven by recurring events that influence the volumes of goods or services consumed. For example, a clothing retailer operates a seasonal business—its sales tend to be higher during the back-to-school and holiday seasons. Changing weather patterns throughout the year also influence levels and types of sales.

The model we built together is an annual model. It captures only the total income a company generates for the year. It sheds no light on the season-to-season variations that affect seasonal businesses such as retailers. To model such a company, consider building a quarterly model instead. It would do a better job of capturing the natural ebb and flow of the company's sales volumes throughout the year. You will have to undertake several adjustments at various places in the model.

II. This model's income statement employs a simplified, one-line revenue account.

Imagine you were building a model for a company called Fortune Brands (NYSE ticker: FO). At the date of this book's publishing, Fortune Brands was a multidivisional company involved in diversified products.

Each of Fortune Brand's divisions has its own sales growth potential, profitability, asset utilization, etc. Your model therefore would benefit from a more detailed treatment of the company's various revenue streams. To analyze a company like Fortune Brands, a so-called "divisional buildup model," which breaks out sales and uses separate drivers for each division, might be appropriate. See Exhibit 5.6.

Exhibit 5.6

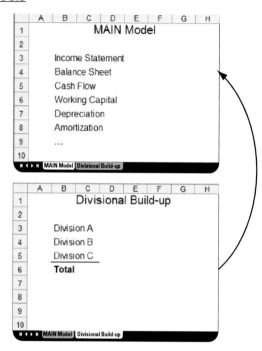

Although we have not formally covered this approach to modeling, hopefully you will recognize in it various elements that are similar to those in to the model you created earlier. For example, the divisional buildup model still benefits hugely from the best practices that we have been advocating. There are references in between sheets that should be color-coded appropriately. The drivers for the divisions will be on the divisional build-up page and those should also be color-coded appropriately. Try to align your data by years. In this example, the same column should be used for all of the projected numbers and drivers. Not to oversimplify things, but once you have seen a few models you have seen them all. We have covered the similar elements in all models throughout the book as part of our best practices.

III. **Although capable, this model is not optimized to perform certain types of analyses. For example, this model would not be able to perform advanced lending modeling or credit analysis.**

The model we built focuses on earnings per share. That is, we built core statements and appropriate supporting schedules with a specific end goal in mind: projecting reasonable, defensible earnings per share for our target company. For that reason, we did not build additional worksheets for analyzing the company's financial statements or credit statistics. There is a lesson to be learned here, which is that a three-statement model can sometimes be modified and enhanced to accommodate your objective. Going through this exercise of customization involves sitting down and thinking about what you will need in order to do this type of analysis.

Using credit analysis as one scenario for customization, let's think about what we would need to do to this model to make it more robust from the standpoint of credit analysis:

• A lender or credit analyst would likely require more detail, especially concerning items on our debt and interest schedule. Recall that, for simplicity, we lumped all of the company's debt and interest-bearing accounts into two categories: revolving credit and long-term debt. That approach allowed for significantly easier modeling. In reality, however, a company's long-term debt is typically comprised of various fixed income securities, such as medium term notes, subordinated notes, and convertible debt. More rigorous lending or credit analyses require more detailed models with greater focus on a company's various debt tranches. We would need to add more detail and more types of debt to our balance sheet and debt and interest schedule. We would also need to re-analyze the 10-K for debt information. But all in all, this is a relatively straightforward exercise. Most of the other model components would remain the same.

• A detailed credit analysis would also involve calculating ratios to analyze the company. One could easily calculate various profitability, coverage, liquidity, and capitalization ratios by using the appropriate items from the model we built together. Indeed, such analyses would employ some of the same line items from the earnings model we created. We would need to create a new ratios page, and use references from the model into the ratios page for these calculations.

Even though the discussion here has centered on the specific demands of credit analysis, the key learning point to grasp is the concept of adapting the model to suit the particular demands of the work you need it to do. Think about what you need to do and what information is already contained in the model. Then make the necessary adjustments where appropriate, and build.

IV. How do I use this model for another company? Using this model as a template.

In the preceding section, we discussed how to customize a model for a specific analysis. What if you wanted to use this model as a template for another company entirely? The good news is that your model is in great shape. The proper color coding means that the drivers, formulas and references are properly identified. Nevertheless, there are some things to consider and some steps to walk through when executing.

The first thing to recognize is that "one size does not fit all." There are a few things to watch when you are modifying this model for a new company. To use this model as a template for a new company:

1) Study the new company's financials
2) Identify any new line items
3) Design the flow-of-funds
   • New line items to and from your core statements
4) Forecast each of the new line items
   • Separate schedule, or just a simple formula?
   • Make sure that any change in the balance sheet is explained by an appropriate change in the cash flow statement.
5) Before deleting anything, hesitate!

With these caveats in mind, the model you have just completed is a fantastic tool for analysis and valuation. Before we dive into specific applications of your model, there is one last important step to perform.

 Please view the Online Companion for related supplementary media.

Matching Consensus EPS

You may recall from our previous discussion of drivers that the assumptions we make in building our model are very important. Selecting appropriate drivers requires an understanding of the business and the industry in which the company operates. Always perform a 'gut' or 'sanity' check to make sure you've chosen drivers that are reasonable and defensible.

Remember the purpose of our model: to analyze and project a public company's earnings per share (EPS). If the company's stock is widely held, then it is likely that a large number of equity research analysts already cover, or are assigned to analyze, the company. Information service providers aggregate these analysts' EPS estimates into what is called a **consensus EPS**. This information reflects what the research community believes a company's EPS will be for the next few years.

Ultimately, the drivers you select for your model will be based on your beliefs about the future of the company. However, you may find it useful to model a separate scenario that matches the consensus EPS. That way, you can compare the output of your assumptions with what the valuation community is thinking. To model a consensus scenario, first identify the variables you can adjust to match consensus estimates for EPS in the first projected year. The

many variables, or drivers, which exist in our model fall into three buckets:

1) Operating assumptions – These assumptions appear on the income statement and were used to forecast our target company's EBITDA. They include: sales growth rate, gross margin, and SG&A margin. Key working capital assumptions, such as accounts receivable days, inventory days, and accounts payable days, could also fall in this category.

2) Investing assumptions – These are used to forecast the company's capital expenditures and purchases of definite life intangibles, such as licenses or patents.

3) Financing assumptions – These are used to model the effects of certain financing activities, such as share repurchases and issuances, the exercise of dilutive securities, and dividend payouts.

Clearly, there are many assumptions and drivers at our disposal. On the one hand, this speaks favorably about the truly flexible, dynamic nature of the model we've built. On the other hand, it makes the exercise of matching the consensus EPS much more complex. To simplify your approach, we suggest starting with operating assumptions. First let's identify the operating drivers on the income statement.

The goal here is to adjust our drivers in a way that is reasonable and defensible and enables us to match consensus EPS in the first projected year. In choosing drivers, consider the following:

- What has the historical trend been in the past? In most recent periods?

- Has the company announced any initiatives that could affect its future performance? What is your hypothesis about the resulting impact of these initiatives?

- Has the company given direct guidance in a press release or maybe in a filing (for example, the discussion in a 10-K or annual report)?

Once our model matches the consensus EPS in the first projected year, we can further align it to the views of the research community by 1) matching the consensus EPS in the second projected year, and 2) matching the consensus five-year EPS compounded annual growth rate (CAGR).

Matching the consensus EPS in the second projected year is a process similar to matching the consensus EPS in the first year. Simply revisit your assumptions and change your drivers to yield the desired EPS value in year two. Changing operating assumptions in year two requires first 'breaking' the flatline logic in Excel to make these assumptions blue input cells, rather than black references.

Matching the consensus five-year EPS CAGR requires modifying the remaining flatline logic being used in years three through five to include a 'step' function. In Excel, a step function can be used to gradually increase or decrease an assumption over a period of years. The 'flatline with a step' adds a degree of precision that enables us to match the EPS growth rate forecasted by analysts.

 Please view the Online Companion for related supplementary media.

Next Steps

Now that we have created a model that matches consensus EPS, what's next? First, you want to make sure that you have run the proper sensitivity analysis. Then you can take this model and apply it to several real-world situations.

Sensitivity Analysis: Data Tables

Since EPS is such an important metric in our analysis, we want to see the correlation between it and our operating drivers. In other words, we want to assess the sensitivity of our company's earnings to fluctuations in operating performance. For example, what would happen to EPS if sales growth were to decrease by 1% each of the next five years? What would happen to EPS growth rate if gross margin were to improve? These are the kinds of questions practitioners will want to answer when evaluating a company.

Fortunately, there is a wonderful tool in Excel called a data table. Data tables allow you to analyze how different values of an **Input Variable** (driver) affect an **Output Cell** (EPS in this example).

Exhibit 5.7

Proj 1 EPS Sensitivity Tables	
One-way, vertical table	
	$2.48
42.4%	$2.40
42.6%	$2.42
42.8%	$2.45
Gross Margin 43.0%	$2.48
43.2%	$2.50
43.4%	$2.53
43.6%	$2.56

In Exhibit 5.7 above, we are examining the impact on projected year 1 EPS given various changes in the gross margin driver. For every increase of 20 basis points (bps) in gross margin, EPS seems to increase by $0.02 - $0.03. Having established this, we now know the risk associated with upwards and downwards movements in gross margin.

After running sensitivities on key drivers, we can now place our model into specific usage contexts by looking at how various professionals would actually employ it.

The following is an introductory discussion of certain types of analysis. If you want a more detailed discussion of DCFs and other valuation techniques, please refer to our corporate valuation course pack. More information can be found at www.ttsuniversity.com.

Buy-side or Investor

Let's say you are a professional asset or fund manager, or even an individual investor considering making an investment in the target company. You can use this model to see what assumptions are required to match consensus EPS estimates. That is, this model helps you to answer the question: What kind of operating performance will the company need to achieve in order to meet the market's earnings expectations?

The utility of building a model that matches consensus is in understanding how the market thinks about the company. How sensitive do you think the market will be to changes in earnings per share? More importantly, do you expect something to happen to the company that is not currently reflected in the share price? With this model in hand, you can now make real-time adjustments to its various drivers to anticipate the impact of any changes in the company's business.

For example, imagine that you believe the company's sales growth rate will increase because of the launch of a hot new product. What is the expected change to sales growth? Can that be sustained? More importantly, assuming the company is being valued based on earnings potential, what is the expected impact to earnings per share?

The usefulness of this model is that it gives you the flexibility to make real-time changes and to expand upon its detail. For example, if you are trying to value a multi-divisional company, then it may be useful to replace the one-line revenue income statement with a divisional buildup model. If you are analyzing a seasonal company or industry, then it may be useful to build a quarterly model instead of an annual model.

Equity Research

Sell-side research analysts are responsible for developing and relaying to the market an investment thesis based on the projected earnings and cash flows of a company. Various professionals, including buy-side professionals and investment bankers, use this information in making business decisions.

Typically, a research report will provide one to three years of projected financials for a company. However, a research analyst will likely have a 'behind the scenes' model that is longer than three years. Although research reports generally emphasize the income statement, most analysts will provide other core statements and analyses in their reports.

Research analysts continuously update their analysis of companies within their coverage universe. They also have discussions with other financial professionals, industry sources, and the management of the company itself to formulate their composite opinion about the company's future performance.

If there is an internal or external event that affects the future of the company, the research analyst will want to develop and convey an opinion to the market in a timely manner. To facilitate this communication, a research analyst will need a well-structured, flexible projections model. Armed with such a model, an analyst can quickly and easily adjust the relevant drivers and visualize the impact of these changes to the company's bottom line.

Industry Finance

If you are an industry professional working within a company, the types of financial models you will create or encounter will vary depending on your department and job function. For example, people close to the product or service line tend to be involved in forecasting. Imagine you work for a retail company and are responsible for forecasting sales for a particular product line. What drives the sales of those products? Is a flatline driver appropriate? Perhaps you should create a revenue buildup schedule that forecasts each product individually, then consolidates those projections into different revenue groups or into a total revenue number.

Similar forecasting techniques and modeling best practices can be applied to budgeting as well. First, identify your drivers and inputs. Once identified, keep your color scheme consistent. That is, blue cells should represent inputs and black cells should represent formulas or references.

Imagine you are the treasurer or CFO of a company. The financial statement analysis found on the ratios page provides a few key metrics for analyzing the overall company. A particular area of interest is the working capital analysis. In our working capital schedule, we analyzed accounts receivable collection and inventory turnover days. It might make sense to calculate turnover and percentage of sales metrics to garner further insights. A CFO might also be interested in the capitalization of the company. Our model utilizes a simplified long-term debt schedule that allows for a basic analysis of debt capitalization. However, if a company has multiple sources of debt, you might consider breaking out its debt by instrument to show different paydown schedules. Adding complexity to the model could be useful for a CFO seeking a clearer picture of her company's leverage.

Sell-side/Investment Bank

The investment banker will primarily use this model to discuss how potential changes in the client's business could lead to changes in EPS.

However, this model could also serve as a useful starting point for an investment banker's valuation of a client's business. That is, a banker might use this model as the primary basis for more specific valuation analyses.

For example, imagine you are a banker trying to generate a preliminary valuation of your client's business. One technique used to value a company is discounted cash flow analysis. You could use the model we created to project the relevant cash flows used to value a company. We will cover this technique in more detail later.

Imagine you have been contracted to help sell your client's company to another buyer. You could use our earnings model to see what assumptions would be necessary to meet equity research consensus, or to see what the projected EPS would be under different scenarios.

If you plan to combine this company with another public company, then the two companies can be analyzed together by combining their EPS's. Using our earnings model as a starting point, a banker might create a merger consequences model that accomplishes this very task.

 **Please view the Online Companion for related supplementary media.**

Discounted Cash Flow Analysis

We have discussed several potential applications of our completed model. And as we said, one of its main uses is to provide a starting point for valuation.

In this section, we will discuss how to apply our earnings model to a discounted free cash flow analysis. Before we begin, let's briefly review how discounted free cash flows are used to value a business.

Discounted cash flow analysis yields the theoretical valuation of a firm. The driving concept behind discounted cash flow analysis is that the value of a company is based on the value of the free cash flows it can generate in the future. This valuation method is also referred to as the Intrinsic Value Approach.

In order to perform a discounted cash flow valuation, you must first estimate the company's future free cash flows over some reasonable number of years, or the **forecast period**. You then obtain the present value of those free cash flows by discounting them using a reasonable risk factor, or discount rate. The discount rate most commonly used is the company's estimated weighted average cost of capital (WACC). The stream of future free cash flows needs to be discounted because $1,000 generated ten years from now is worth considerably less than $1,000 today. Discounted cash flow analysis therefore, is firmly rooted in the basic concept of the time value of money. A rational investor is assumed to prefer $990 today to $1,000 ten years from now.

The final step is to add the sum of the discounted free cash flows from the forecast period to a dollar figure that represents the terminal value of the company. This terminal value captures the free cash flows that are assumed to occur after the forecast period. The present value of the forecasted free cash flows, together with the present value of the terminal value, yields the company's total estimated enterprise value. That, in a nutshell, is discounted cash flow analysis.

In summation, we can see that a discounted cash flow valuation has three basic components:

- Free cash flows, or more precisely, unlevered free cash flows (UFCFs)

- A terminal value for the company (TV)

- A discount rate, called the weighted average cost of capital, which we will use to discount the future free cash flows and the terminal value to their present values (WACC)

How to derive the third of these components, an appropriate discount rate, is an exercise beyond the scope of this book. Please refer to the TTS corporate valuation course pack for more information. Here, we focus on the other two components of a discounted free cash flow analysis.

 Please view the Online Companion for related supplementary media.

Unlevered Free Cash Flow

Let's look at how to derive the first component, the unlevered free cash flows (UFCFs). Unlevered free cash flows are free cash flows that are independent of the company's capital structure. That is, they are independent of how the company's assets have been financed. They are the company's cash flows before interest expense has been subtracted, which means they are available to all of the firm's capital holders, not just the equity shareholders. Exhibit 5.8 is a typical calculation of UFCFs:

Exhibit 5.8

EBITDA

    Less: Depreciation & amortization

= EBIT

    Less: Taxes

= Tax-effected EBIT

    + Depreciation & amortization

    - Capital expenditures and Additions to Intangibles

    +/- Changes in net working capital

    +/- Changes in other non-cash items

= Unlevered Free Cash Flow

Do a quick inventory of what you need in order to calculate UFCFs and compare that to what you currently have in your model. Do you have EBITDA? Sure! We forecasted that on the income statement. We also have depreciation and amortization from their respective schedules. The rest of the components you need can be referenced from our model into a DCF spreadsheet. Once we have the unlevered free cash flows forecasted, we can discount them to derive their present value.

Terminal Value Calculation

Note, however, that our projections terminate after five, maybe ten years. How, then, do we capture the value of the business beyond the projection period?

Finance professionals use a terminal value to capture the value of the company's cash flows beyond the forecast period. In fact, for a company like Amazon, for example, which posted losses for its first several years as a start-up, the terminal value calculation can be especially important. Two methods are widely used to project the terminal value:

> **A. The Exit Multiple Method** – Assumes that, at the end of the forecast period, the company is worth (or can be "sold for") a multiple of an operating metric (for example, Enterprise Value / EBITDA multiple).
>
> **Terminal value$_N$ = Multiple x Financial metric$_N$,** where N equals the final year of the forecast period.
>
> **B. The Perpetuity Growth Rate Method** – Assumes the company's UFCFs will grow at a moderate, constant rate indefinitely.

$$\text{Terminal Value} = \frac{FCF_n \times (1+g)}{(r-g)}$$

FCF$_n$ = normalized free cash flow in period $_n$

g   = nominal perpetual growth rate

r   = discount rate

The terminal value is expressed in future dollars. Just as future cash flows must be discounted, the terminal value must also be discounted to derive its present value.

The present value of the unlevered free cash flows plus the present value of the terminal value implies the **enterprise value** of a firm. To derive the firm's **equity value**, subtract the value of its net debt, minority interest, and preferred stock. To derive the firm's equity value per share, divide the firm's equity value by its number of shares outstanding.

But don't let yourself get lost in the details. The overall point of this discussion is to demonstrate that the basic earnings model we created can be used as the foundation for more technical valuation techniques. Once an earnings model is completed you've done most of the heavy work. At that point, the amount of additional time and effort it takes to generate valuation analyses is less than you may think. Most of the DCF worksheet, for example, is comprised of green references and black calculations that build upon our completed model. The heavy lifting is already done.

5.3 CONCLUSION

There are a lot of concepts and techniques to think through when building a financial model, but you should not be daunted by the task! The fact that there is no "correct" approach for doing everything should be viewed as a tremendous opportunity—a chance to tailor your approach and fashion your model in a way that best suits your purposes. We hope you'll go forward from here, confident in the techniques you've learned in this book, with a few key takeaways in mind.

First, remember that effective modelers possess a blend of skills:

- Understanding of the company's industry and operations

- Accounting

- Corporate finance

- Excel

Applying these skills effectively requires equal measures of patience of practice. Over time, and with persistence, you will become a proficient modeler whose models are:

- Realistic, reasonable, and defensible

- Flexible, adaptable, and dynamic

- Easy-to-follow, efficient, and clear

Remember that when it comes to modeling, there is no single right answer. But if you are confident and consistent in your approach, others will be compelled to trust your analysis and value your work. That is, perhaps, the best compliment a master modeler can receive. We hope we have armed you with all the valuable insight and modeling best practices you need to guide you on your way to becoming one. So good luck, and get going—the rest is up to you.

 Please view the Online Companion for related supplementary media.